Bumpy Roads

My 35 Year Journey from High School to College Graduation

Jayna Burch

Bee Bold Books

The events and conversations in this book have been set down to the best of the author's ability, although some names and details have been omitted to protect the privacy of individuals.

ISBN 978-1-960129-01-7 *(Paperback)*
ISBN 978-1-960129-00-0 *(ebook)*
First Edition: April 2023

Bee Bold Books
PO Box 176
Weston, TX 75009

www.jaynaburch.com

This is dedicated to all my friends and family that have supported me along this journey. It may not always have been easy to be on this journey with me, but I love you all for being there for me in the good times and the bad. I can not say thank you enough to each of you.

I also want to thank all my professors, Phi Theta Kappa advisors, administrators, and of course, my boss Stephen and all my student employees in Student Engagement at Collin College for assisting in my success as a student and encouraging me as an author and motivational speaker. I truly could not have done all this without you.

Experience is the best teacher. A compelling story is a close second.

— Paul Smith

Contents

Introduction xi
Graduation Speech xv

1. Flat Tires 1
2. Speed Bumps 15
3. Potholes and Detours 31
4. Roadblock 50
5. Speed Bumps 64
6. Getting Lost 75
7. Sightseeing 85
8. New Roadblocks 93
9. Cruising 103
10. Breakdown 114
11. The Fork in the Road 121
12. Driving in Storms 125
13. You Have Arrived at Your Destination? 138
14. Reflections 143

Epilogue 149
Souvenirs of my Journey 153
Photo Album 157
In Memoriam 162

About the Author 165
How Can You Help? 167

Introduction

How Did I Get Here?

Who and I? Why am I writing this? How did I get here? Well, those are good questions, and it is an interesting story. First, I should introduce myself. Hello, I'm Jayna. I am what they call a non-traditional student, which is a student in college after a break of several years, and I just got my Associate's Degree – 35 years after graduating from high school. That in itself is not unique. How I finally got here is, though. This was a very difficult journey to get here. Why I'm writing this is also a bit unique.

The week before classes started, I had a dream. Not once, but 5 nights in a row. The same dream, over and over. I was giving a speech at graduation. The exact same speech every night. This was very weird to me. I was a mediocre student in high school and never had a reason to be giving a graduation speech. I wasn't sure what to make of this dream. It stuck with me. I was constantly thinking about it. And I don't mean I thought about it the next day or for a week or two. I mean, I thought about it all the time until graduation.

Fast forward to 2020. The global pandemic, Covid-19, prevented graduation. After 35 years, it was important to me to be able to walk across the stage and receive my diploma. I stretched it out another semester, hoping Spring 2021 would allow a proper graduation. It didn't. While in college, though, I had gotten very involved in the Phi Theta Kappa International Honor Society. When the college still didn't have a graduation, even though some other colleges did have one, we five officers decided to have a small ceremony for just the few of us officers that were graduating. It was held in the basement of the local historic courthouse. It had just the five of us and our families in person. We also set up a Zoom call for anyone else that wanted to watch us graduate. My ex-husband wore his Ph.D. robes to present our diplomas (curled-up certificate paper with blue bows), and then I gave the graduation speech. The same speech I had dreamed about back in 2018.

After graduation was over, people in person and on Zoom were telling me how inspiring and inspirational my speech was. I took this to heart. In fact, this got me to do some serious thinking. I thought about how I had helped others find their voice and speak up about personal issues over the years. I thought about all the times someone has shared their stories with me, even when they didn't think they could share with others. I thought about what more I could do. Helping people and defending those that can't defend themselves has always been a primary motivator in my life. It even is what encouraged me to share my journey here, to share what I learned along the way, and help others navigate their own journeys. I will warn you, though; this can be a very difficult story to hear.

Since this all started with my speech, I wanted to include it here. *If you don't want spoilers for the rest of the book, skip straight to Chapter 1.* If you would like a roadmap of where we will be going, turn the page and keep on reading. Either way, we will be on this journey together.

Graduation Speech

Graduation Speech: May 2021

Welcome to all of our family and friends that are here to celebrate our graduation from Collin College. This may be a small graduation ceremony, but it means the world to each of us that you are with us tonight.

First, let me say that I'm not speaking to you tonight because I have the best grades or am the most accomplished. Far from it. I'm here with four other amazing, smart, talented, and accomplished individuals whom I have the privilege of knowing and serving in Phi Theta Kappa with. Each of us has been on a journey that has brought us here tonight.

Think of the journey as a highway. Some people took the fastest possible route. They jumped in their cars and sped their way here. They didn't stop along the way. They had a destination to get to, so they put the peddle to the meddle, and they got here as fast as they could.

Others took a more scenic route. They got on the freeway but exited here and there along the way. They took time to see the sights and fill up with gas, maybe even stopping at a cute diner to eat. A more relaxed way to travel. But they still got here.

Finally, there are those of us that tried to speed our way here, but had to stop for flat tires, ran out of gas, had detours, and even got lost trying to get back to the highway. This ended up being my journey, and I'd like to share it with you. I will warn you, though; this may be a difficult one to hear.

When I was a senior in high school, I thought I had it all planned out. I was going to head to Wright State University in Dayton, Ohio. I had my first flat tire before I even got out of high school, though.

Two things made me unprepared for this journey. My first flat tire came in November of my senior year when one of my best friends was diagnosed with cancer on her spine.

The next time my car broke down was harder to fix. I had been extremely active in school, as you can see from my school jacket. I did not play sports but was involved in something every season. I was a statistician, manager, cheerleader, band, and choir, during football, basketball, soccer, and tennis. Then in April, with only about 6 weeks left in high school, I was sexually assaulted by one of my teachers. I became a wallflower, and my grades took a dive. It didn't help that they let this teacher back in the school and threatened me if I said anything.

Needless to say, I wasn't in the best place mentally when I got back on the road to college. My grades suffered. Then I made a stop to help fellow travelers. I found out that that teacher had done the same thing before. I had been told there was "no physical proof, no witnesses, and nothing in his past history to indicate such a thing." This was a small town, and the police had "lost" my police report. When found out that this girl had been told the same exact thing. And since they didn't bother to put her accusation in his record, there was nothing there to protect me. In fact, they gave him another 5-year contract and a raise!

I decided that the girls needed to be protected, so I set out to do all that I could. I armed myself with our local reporter, the Dayton Daily News, Channel 7 News, and my attorney (to keep me from saying anything to get myself in trouble). I went to the school board meeting and got it on the record. Plus, it was now in the press. In the future, there may be no physical proof or witnesses, but there WAS going to be a record of his past behavior, and everyone had been warned.

All of this took its toll on me, though, and I was put on academic probation. I left Wright State Spring of '87.

Well, I got back on the road the next fall and, this time headed for Sinclair Community College. There were a few detours on this road too. Right before school started, my cousin committed suicide. This was very hard on me, but I got on the road and started classes. Life was good, and I made new friends and was getting decent grades. Then the next detour hit as my friend from high school passed away from her cancer. That detour turned into me getting lost when a couple of months later, I got abducted from the Dayton Mall and raped. The first victim in a series of rapes. All this and I had just turned 20 years old.

I figured Ohio wasn't a safe place for me and set out on a new road. I made plans to move back to Missouri, where my extended family all lived. This was a much better road to be on, or so I thought. I had new friends, 2 jobs that I liked, and was looking at going to Southwest Missouri State University. But before I could register for classes, I hit a huge pothole in the road. One month, my roommate moved out on the 1st with no notice, leaving me stuck with her half of the rent and a $600 phone bill. I couldn't pay my bills, and my phone got disconnected. So, I *called my mom and said if she still wanted me to move to Texas, come and get me.*

So, 2 weeks before my 22nd birthday, I got on the road to here. I was on a very different road this time, but I figured this was the road I was supposed to be on. I moved here on a Tuesday, picked up Wednesday's newspaper and made a few calls, had two job interviews Thursday and had a job offer by Friday. I got my bills paid off and got back out on my own. I got on my road of life, climbing the corporate ladder.

I did try and go back to college once, but life just kept happening. It was jobs, marriage, kids, volunteer work, etc. This was my road, and it was a good road.

Fast forward to 2017. My youngest son was graduating high school and about to head out on his road to college at UTD. I went to the college one day to pick up a UTD t-shirt for his senior photos. It was a beautiful spring day. I could hear the kids playing soccer and tennis. I was watching the kids walking to classes and lying in the grass studying. It was almost like a scene from a movie. By the time I got back to my car, I was in tears. That was what I had wanted. What I had missed out on. Richard said to me, "so what are you going to do about it?"

What was I going to do? Simply get on a new road to a new destination. I learned I could get a scholarship from my company that would cover all my college expenses here at Collin College. So, with the support of my family, I got on this road to college and to this graduation. It wasn't a very smooth road as I still worked full time, was a full-time student, and still needed to have time for my family, but it was a much better journey. For the first time in my life, I was an honor student and decided to make the most of my college experience by joining Phi Theta Kappa. I am so glad I did. I got to meet amazing people, like these and had the opportunity to work on CougarThon twice. This year, in fact, I *was privileged to get to organize CougarThon, where we raised over $7051 for the Children's Miracle Network (and that was virtual during a global pandemic!). I am so proud to be a part of this group and will forever call each of them my friend.*

I will never regret a single mile of my journey. It has made me the person I am today. It has given me the strength, wisdom, and maturity to set goals and work to achieve them. It is MY road and MY journey.

Our travels don't end here. If you will all look under your seats, you will find a roadmap. This is just a reminder that we all can choose our destinations, plan what roads to travel, and can even find some wonderful sights to see along the way. We will all take different roads to different places from here. I only hope we keep in touch so we can share the excitement of our journeys along the way.

Bon Voyage, everyone.

Wait! What? Did that say that after everything I went through that, I wouldn't change anything? Not a single thing? Yes. Yes, it did. This journey has taught me so much about who I am, who I want to be, and how I can better help others. It has made me the person I am today. I am excited to share my journey with you, the good and the bad. It's all important in how it shaped me.

Chapter 1

Flat Tires

I had moved around a lot as a child. By the time I was 9 years old, I had already lived in six cities in four different states. That is when I arrived in Bellbrook. This was a small town of about 3,000 people. My parents quickly realized that all this moving was taking a toll on me as I was struggling to make friends anymore. Why should I if I was just going to move again? Because the moving was having a negative effect on me, my parents made the tough decision to tell my dad's company that they needed to not move us again. Not at least until I graduated high school. That is how I ended up in this small town.

Before I go any further, I need to give some background on my high school days. I was smart enough but didn't really care about my grades. I just kept my grades good enough to stay out of trouble at home. Classes were just what you went to while waiting for all the fun extra-curricular activities after school. I was a student assistant to a couple of the teachers and was also a library aid. I was in the band and the choir. I was in the Audio/Visual Club and French Club. While I have no athletic talent when it comes to sports, I was a soccer statistician for a year, and I was a freshman basketball statistician, and then a JV basketball cheerleader for a year. Plus I also videotaped all the home basketball games for three years. For the men's tennis team, I was the statistician/equipment manager for four years. The list goes on and on. My school jacket was filled with my varsity letters, pins, and chevrons, despite not actually playing any sports.

Being very mature for my age, I liked the extra responsibility I was given. In fact, I was the kind of student that was even allowed to grade her own test because I was honest with my scores. This is what made school bearable for me. But even with all of this, I had always felt like an outsider because I wasn't born in this little town, as the other kids constantly reminded me. All this extra responsibility made me feel included and as if I did belong there.

In high school, I did have three extremely close friends. I met Samantha when I moved to Bellbrook back in fourth grade. By middle school, we did just about everything together. Her mom was like a second mom to me. We did so much together and spent a lot of weekends at each other's houses. Her mom even started a garden club that Samantha and I were in, and had fun going to competitions together. In fact, Samantha and I even got to be on our local TV station's morning show, where we both made a flower arrangement during the segment. On weekends, we could start a game of UNO on Friday night and end it somewhere on Sunday afternoon after church!

Steve and I became friends the next year in fifth grade. He was teased a lot in school due to his weight, and during indoor recess, I noticed he played alone. Because of this, I would grab a board game and go over and play with him. This started a lifelong friendship. The two of us had season passes to Kings Island in high school, and he was one of my roommates in college. We did so much together.

Kim moved to Bellbrook in the middle of our sophomore year of high school. Coming from a very different school environment from Bellbrook's, she was always sitting alone, so I started sitting by her and welcomed her as a friend. Bellbrook was an idyllic kind of school with very little drugs or violence and not even a teenage pregnancy till one my senior year. Kim had gone to the only school in the area with a metal detector, plus a lot of gang and drug issues at that time. I'm sure it was a culture shock when she came to Bellbrook High School. She very much felt out of place. That is how we became the best of friends. We learned to drive together and learned to swim together. You would have thought we had known each other our whole lives.

I used to think you needed a lot of friends and be popular or in the "In" crowd, but honestly, having 3 people in your life that you love and care for and that care for you is all one really needs.

My senior year, as high school was nearing its end, it was time to get ready for college. I thought I had planned well for my journey to college. In my junior year, I researched colleges, took my SATs, applied to my local college of choice, which was Wright State University, and had been accepted. I was excited to go to college. It was going to be a new adventure, and honestly, I was looking forward to getting out of Bellbrook. Even though I had been there since fourth grade, I was constantly told I wasn't "from" Bellbrook. I craved a feeling of being where I belonged. Luckily, Steve was going to be going to Wright State too! Unfortunately, though, before I could start out on my college journey, I had my first two flat tires.

In November of my senior year, Kim fell one day after school. Her legs just gave out on her, and she collapsed. Tests were done, and she was diagnosed with cancer on her spine. She ended up having surgery to remove the tumor, but it was so entwined in the nerves that they could only take out about 90% of it. I dedicated time to visiting her at the hospital and then visiting her at home. I knew what she was doing in physical therapy, so I could help her. She did not want anyone at school to know so they wouldn't feel sorry for her. When she could finally come back to school, I left my classes early so I could get her from her class and take her to her next class before the halls got crowded. By this time, she was out of a wheelchair but was supposed to be using a cane. She refused and just had me help support her as she walked between classes. I never minded. I was happy to be helping her during her recovery, but at 17 years old, it's also a surreal experience to have one of your friends suffering from cancer.

The year before, her dad had died of cancer. This probably is why her family made some of the choices it did. At first, her family tried to hide it from her. She was told she had a tumor, but it wasn't malignant and that it was being removed, and the radiation treatments were just a precaution. Steve and I had been told the truth while she was still in the hospital but told not to let her know. I didn't agree with this as she had just turned 19 years old. I felt she had a right to know what was going on with her body, but I did respect the family's decision and promised her family that I wouldn't tell her. Well, one Saturday afternoon after she had finished the radiation treatments, we were hanging out in her room. She was still too tired to get out of bed, but we hung out in her room with me changing records and stuff. Kim didn't really even sit up, but she was thrilled to have company. She was so excited that her hair was starting to grow back. It was like peach fuzz coming in, and she wanted me to see and feel it. Well, I honestly couldn't see it yet, but I could feel it a bit when I rubbed her head. Then she said to me, "You know I have cancer, don't you?" "Yes," I replied. "When did they tell you?" She looked me in the eyes and replied, "You just did."

Her family was so mad at me for letting her know when they found out. Sorry, not sorry. First, I didn't really tell her. I was just tricked into confirming it. Second, she had a right to know what was going on with her body. In fact, she did know. She just couldn't get her family to tell her the truth. This is why she felt she had to trick me into telling her. To this day, I'm still not sorry it happened, though.

She was trying to hide that she had cancer when we went back to school, and I did my best to keep her secret. Kim did not want people to feel sorry for her, and I understood and respected that. I stayed strong for her, as I would do anything to protect her. I had always been one to stand up to protect my friends, as I knew all too well how much it hurt to be teased or bullied. I tried to protect my friend from that as much as possible. As far as hiding the cancer, we were successful in this for most of the year.

Sadly, this wasn't even the worst part of my senior year.

A few months later, in April, which was less than two months before graduation, I was sexually assaulted by a teacher at the school. To this day, I still speak in as general terms as possible, just as I was forced to back then. I think this comes from being threatened to keep quiet about it when I was still young and easy to intimidate. I'm learning now that I do have a voice. Though I am free to speak about it freely and do, I still will not name the teacher here, as it's not really important as he is now retired. I will also NOT give any details about the assault itself as I don't want to trigger anyone reading this. Those that needed to know at the time know.

This assault hit me hard! I think the worse part to deal with was when I discovered that I had basically been chosen my freshman year and groomed by him over the next four years. He gained my trust by being given extra responsibilities and for him fighting for my varsity letter, and fighting to allow me to ride the team bus since I was as important to the team as the athletes. I wasn't old enough or mature enough to understand just how cruel some people can be. I didn't see any red flags. How a person thinks it's ok to use and manipulate someone for their own personal pleasure, not caring about the damage they can do, still astonishes me to this day. Let me back up a bit and tell you what happened from the beginning.

In my freshman year, I had this teacher for the last period of the day. By the time I got to class, it had been a while since lunch, so I tended to get the shakes and get light-headed. He had been so understanding. The first time it happened, I had to call my mom to pick me up. He had told her and I that I could sit in the back of the room and it was okay to tuck a few snacks into my desk and eat them in class if needed. I saw this as being compassionate and understanding.

As I was a good student and was hanging out at the tennis courts since I had friends on the team, he asked me to be the statistician and equipment manager. I was thrilled. The only thing was, at that time, I could only go to home matches, and for the away matches, he would bring me the results, and I would record them and keep the books. In my sophomore year, I started driving to some of the away matches with Steve. Next, he fought to get me a varsity letter for the work I had done. The last week of school he gave it to me! In my junior year, he didn't want me driving myself to matches and fought to have me travel with the team. Another win. I was thrilled at how respected I was. Well, that's what I thought it was, anyway.

I will say that I actually had a warning that something was wrong, but didn't see it for what it was - a warning. One day it had been raining, and since the tennis courts were just six houses down the road and through a path in the woods, I would normally just walk. Because of the rain, though, the path would have been extremely muddy, and my car wasn't working that week. The coach offered to pick me up and take me to the courts. That is not too weird in itself.

We got to the courts ahead of everyone. While waiting for the rest of the team to show up, he said he was going to lie down in the back. I was still in the passenger seat, and the keys were on the turn signal. It wasn't raining anymore, but since it had rained all day, there were puddles of water all over the courts. All of a sudden, my angels, as I now call them, appeared and were screaming for me to get out of the van. I didn't know why, as nothing seemed out of the ordinary. But I could hear them in my head screaming for me to get out as loud as if they were standing right next to me. This was a new experience as it had never happened to me before. I looked out the windows, and none of the guys were there yet, so I decided to listen to my angels. I just grabbed the keys and said I was going down to unlock and clean off the courts. The coach just said, "Okay". As soon as I got out of the van, my angels got quiet again. It was such a weird experience.

A couple of weeks later is when my life got turned upside

down. We had to postpone several tournaments due to him missing school and matches due to family issues. After one of the away matches once he returned, he said I needed to go with him to the bus barn when he returned the bus as I had the new schedule and needed to drop it off so the bus could be reserved.

The bus barn wasn't even around the high school. It was behind what had been the football field at one of our elementary schools, as it was once the old high school. Picture an old 3-story high school turned elementary school, in a small downtown area, kinda behind a church. Beside this was a single-story extension at a 90-degree angle to the main building. Behind these buildings was a large blacktop playground with lots of games like four-square courts and tether ball courts, swing sets, jungle gyms, etc. Behind all this is a large field, the former football field. In the back to the side of the field was the bus barn.

This trapped me after hours in a place where there was not a single person around at about 6:30 pm. As I said earlier, I won't go into any specific details as to what happened as it is not necessary, and I don't want to trigger anyone reading this that has gone through anything similar. Just suffice it to say that a death grip on the seat in front of me kept it from being anything worse than just what is legally called "gross sexual imposition". I barely escaped from being raped. The emotional toll was just as great, though. Once he realized I was fighting back and he didn't want to risk it any further, he drove me back to the high school where my car was.

I really didn't know how to handle things. There were a million emotions all hitting me at once. Fear was my initial reaction while it was happening, not knowing if or how I could get out of the predicament I was in. Anger quickly followed, especially as he told me to keep this "just between us" as I got out of his van and into my car. I remember beating my hand on my steering wheel, cursing him all the way home. At the same time came an overwhelming feeling of sickness, like I could throw up any minute. I was so hurt and betrayed by someone whom I looked up to that I just couldn't wrap my head around all this. My whole body was trembling. This, I'm sure, was me being anxious as to what was going to happen next, or could have just been my brain being completely overloaded with emotions. I can't remember any time before this that I had experienced this many emotions all at the same time. In a way, I felt completely out of control. I just knew I needed to get myself pulled together before I got home.

When I got home, mom was cooking, and I just said we had stopped at McDonald's and didn't need dinner. I went to my room, and I called Kim and told her what happened. She had just started driving again and said she had to drop off her nephew, then would be on her way over, but she also said that I needed to tell my mom and dad before she got there. That is such a hard conversation to start. It's not something you just blurt out. I was so nervous and nauseous. Once I told my parents, I went back to my room to wait for Kim.

By this point, I have gone completely numb. I was so physically, mentally, and emotionally exhausted by this point. I could hear my mom calling the principal and superintendent on the phone while I was waiting for Kim and sitting at my computer. I could not go out there and be a part of that. I needed to kind of hide in my room where I felt safe. When Kim got there, I heard my parents tell her quickly what had happened, and she pretended not to know. After Kim left, my dad came in and put 2 rolls of 35mm film on the desk, saying this was a replacement for the roll he borrowed and one extra as interest. Honestly, my dad was trying. He just didn't know what to say, and I don't blame him, but he felt he needed to say something. Photography was something we enjoyed together, so it was all that he could say. I understood that he was trying to say he cared. I just went to bed after that and cried myself to sleep.

I took the next day off of school so I could rest and relax. Then later that day, my parents and I went to the police station and filed a police report.

After the attack, I went from being this outgoing, energetic person to a wallflower. I felt violated, sad, angry, depressed, and betrayed. If being sexually assaulted wasn't bad enough, I was shut down by everyone that was supposed to protect me. I had tried to report this to the police, but unfortunately, this is where being in a small town is a bad thing. Everyone knew everyone, including the police chief and the superintendent. When I went to pick up a copy of my police report, I was told that they had lost the police report! My parents and I also reported it to the school. The school, both principals and superintendent, told me that there was "no physical proof, no witnesses, and nothing in his past history to indicate such a thing".

In fact, we were asked to come to a meeting at the school with the superintendent and the teacher. We asked if we should have legal counsel with us, and we were told no, this is an informal meeting. HA! This was actually a meeting with the Superintendent and the school's lawyer, the teacher and his two lawyers, and us, without any legal assistance since we were told we didn't need one. To make matters worse, his attorneys threatened my parents and me with libel and slander if we told anyone or said anything. They tried to fake pictures of what the inside of the van looked like and that it was "impossible". Yea, if you stage the photos before you take them!!! My dad sat there with his fists balled up in his pockets at how I was being treated, threatened, and bullied, but could not do anything to stop it at that time.

Then the teacher was allowed back into the school without the school even giving me the courtesy of letting me know in advance to prepare myself. Imagine my surprise when I saw the van that I had been locked in sitting there in the teacher's parking lot one morning as I was getting off the bus! I was so upset that I went straight to one of the counselor's offices to call my parents. I didn't even stop to say good morning to anyone. I just made a straight shot to the office. This counselor also betrayed my trust and told my attacker everything I said to her.

It was all way too much for me, and I completely shut down. I was being bullied by my own school administration! I was still having to help Kim at school, but there was no one helping me. How could they? No one was allowed to know. The guys on my team kept asking me why I had abandoned them, which made me feel even worse. The school had banned not only the teacher but banned me from the tennis courts as well, but I couldn't even say that. I couldn't tell them anything. Two of the guys were in percussion with me, and they were both curious and worried about me. They knew something was up, but I'm sure no one in their wildest dreams would have guessed what it was. One day they would sit down next to me, one on each side of me, against the back band room doors, and try to get me to talk. They came right out and asked me why I abandoned them. I said nothing. Then they asked what was going on, and I literally did not say a single word because if I even tried to talk, I would have ended up crying. I started trembling, and I had to get up and run out of the room before the tears started.

My closest cry for help was asking my Psychology teacher if I could change my term paper topic from anorexia nervosa and bulimia to the psychological effects of rape on a victim. Since this teacher had me all four years for homeroom, two years of English, and was the JV basketball coach (I had been a JV basketball cheerleader), as well as my Psychology teacher, he knew me very well. He had seen the change in my personality. He, too, wanted more information, but that was the only information that I could give him. I was choking up as I was talking to him, so he knew something serious was up. I think at first, before I asked to change my topic, he thought it was the pressure of dealing with Kim as the staff knew about her cancer. I knew he was worried about me too, but I was still being threatened by the teacher's lawyers and the school, so no matter how desperately I wanted to, I could not say a thing. Needless to say, my teacher let me change my term paper topic. Mr. Yux was always one of my favorite teachers and forever will be.

As a further slap in the face by the school, they gave my attacker another five-year contract and a raise! Can you believe that! They truly cared more about their school's reputation than the safety of their students! By the time graduation came, I was just a shell of my former self. Every adult that was supposed to protect me, except my parents, did the exact opposite. They abandoned me, or worse, they threatened and bullied me. I could no longer trust the people around me.

Due to all this, I felt that I had no voice, no recourse. Back then, most rape/sexual assault victims didn't have much of a voice. The media didn't report it like it does today. There were also many people that would blame the victim. This kept victims from reporting it or even telling friends or family. There was very much of a stigma in being a rape/sexual assault victim in the 1980s. In my case, that was amplified by a school that not only wasn't protecting me, but they, in fact, were protecting him and allowed my attacker to threaten me. I graduated in June of 1986, and I was so glad to be going to college and getting out of that town as fast as I could. The college I was going to, Wright State, was just down the road from this little town, so many of the students I went to school with would also be there. I would just have to do my best to distance myself from them as I still could not let anyone know what happened.

I couldn't even be excited for my graduation, even though that was a celebration of the end of my time at Bellbrook High School. Kim had worked very hard in physical therapy to be able to walk at school and at graduation without assistance. For the Baccalaureate ceremony, it was held in a bit older church. We started by walking down a flight of simple wooden stairs to the basement, relined up, and had to walk back up those same stairs before entering the door at the front of the sanctuary. I had been lined up in front of her so she could hold on to me and Steve was behind her to hold her up and keep her from falling. She had been offered to just sit in the front row and join us as we were walking in, but again, she didn't want anyone to know something was wrong. Unfortunately, this was very tiring for her, and Kim fell at the Baccalaureate ceremony, right at the front of the Church in front of everyone as we walked in front of the pulpit. She was so mortified. After that, she never got out of her wheelchair again, not even if we were just going out to a movie or something. She even graduated in her wheelchair. It's so sad to see someone that young completely giving up like that.

Finally, I graduated and was able to leave Bellbrook for the last time. In an ironic twist, I got a speeding ticket on my last trip out of town. In fact, I was just 5 houses away from the main road out of town. It was like they had to hurt me one more time before they would let me go. At least I left, and I didn't look back. It would take 35 years before I stepped foot back in Bellbrook again.

Chapter 2

Speed Bumps

Fall arrived and I started at Wright State University, trying my best to put things behind me and make a fresh start. Steve and I went to orientation at Wright State about a week or two before classes started. After we went to a couple of presentations and found where our classes would be, we went out to the quad. It was such a beautiful day. Sunny but not too hot. There were also a couple of big old trees around, giving shade. Many of the student organizations, all the Greek chapters, and lots of campus groups had tables set up around the quad, giving out information and recruiting new members. Steve and I got to go repelling down the side of one of the buildings with the ROTC (well, I went repelling, and Steve waited at the bottom for me) and got to see so many activities I could get involved with. This gave me things to look forward to, and I thought I was prepared to go ahead and put things behind me and embark on my new college journey. One of the organizations there was the college radio station. I spoke with the students from the radio station, and it sounded like fun, so I thought I'd give radio a try. I'm so glad I did, but more on that later.

Once orientation was over, we drove down to pick up Steve's car at the mechanic not too far from campus. The mechanic was at the bottom of a hill on a very busy road where we would have to stop and wait to turn left with no turn bay. This very busy street was right beside Wright Patterson Air Force Base and Wright State University, so there was a lot of traffic, even though it was early in the afternoon. I looked into the rearview mirror just long enough to see a car coming, and it didn't look like it was slowing or stopping. For a brief moment, everything seems to be in slow motion. I was watching but didn't have time to say anything to Steve. That was probably a good thing, so he didn't tense up like I was. Sure enough, a woman, who was speeding and didn't see me in time, hit me from behind. There was a loud crunch of metal sound as we were whipped forward and back. She was in an old El Camino with a plywood back window with a circle cut out to see out. I drove a much smaller 1976 Dodge Colt. My car was totaled, but it was still drivable.

When she got out of her car, she was yelling at us, but luckily the guys at the mechanic's place called the police for us. This was my first real accident and was shocked, and I was hurt but tried to do what I was told and not argue with her. Just get the insurance information, I told myself. She never gave it to me, just yelled at me. Once the police got there, she yelled at the officer for taking too long and making her late for her appointment at the tattoo parlor. Due to her making such a fuss, they didn't even talk to me till they finished with her and let her go. My back hurt and my legs were shaky, and I was feeling like I could collapse. The longer I waited, the worse it got. I was leaning over what was left of the trunk of my car as I was struggling to stand anymore.

It wasn't till the police officer was finished taking my statement that he offered to call for an ambulance. I told him that Steve could probably get me to the hospital before the ambulance could even get there. The officer didn't even argue with me, just said fine, and he left. I have never before or since had such a bad encounter with the police. The officer was rude and really acted like he didn't want to be there and didn't care if he helped us or not.

We parked my car and got into Steve's car, and he drove me to the hospital. By the time we got there and parked, I couldn't stand up. In fact, I could barely feel my legs. Steve was trying to help me walk through the parking garage and into the ER. The sweetest old man, that was a volunteer at the hospital, saw me and grabbed a wheelchair, and ran over to me. He helped me into the wheelchair and pushed me into the ER. I was taken back pretty quickly, which was kinda surprising, honestly.

Once back in an exam room, they would not allow Steve back to see me since he was not family. He was nervous for me since he didn't know what was going on. Well, my family wasn't in the area anymore as they had moved a couple of hours away to Indianapolis, so they weren't there either. I was scared because, by now, I couldn't feel my legs at all. In fact, I was just lying in the bed, trying to count the tiny little holes in the acoustic tiles on the ceiling to take my mind off what was going on. They sent in a counselor, and he was more irritating than helpful. I really just wanted him to leave.

Luckily a few hours later, the feeling started to return to my legs, and I got to go home. It was a pinched nerve due to a slight twist in a vertebra. While this incident was over, it would lead to a lifetime of back issues. In case you are curious, no, the woman did not have insurance. It was my uninsured motorist insurance that had to cover everything, including my totaled car. This was NOT the way to start my new college journey!

Back to the radio station. My happy place at that time. I started out by doing sports. This is NOT my strong suit. It was hockey season, and I was struggling with all the hockey players' names. Even though the Associated Press printed out the phonetic spellings of the names, I was still struggling. After talking with the different directors, I switched to the news department, where I was much better suited.

As a bonus, the morning jazz DJ taught me how to spin records, and he even created my own radio soap opera, "Life with Jayna". We spoofed every aspect of my life, and I was able to laugh again. Instead of being from Missouri, my character was from Hog Trough, Iowa. My roommate (more on her in a bit) worked there, so her character was Daisy Spikes, and her boyfriend, who was the sports director, was Thrash Slasher. It was so funny!!! I loved going in with the jazz DJ in the mornings since he would let me pick my own playlist and cue up my own records. I really felt at home in the radio station. Everyone there was so much fun.

Even when not working, I liked to hang out there with all my new friends. There were times there were so many of us in the lobby that it was standing-room only. You never knew what was going to happen there or who would be in. Once, the Jolt Cola rep came in and gave us a couple of cases of Jolt Cola. Oh my gosh, people were drinking at least one, if not two, or three cans in less than an hour. Everyone was bouncing off the walls, and the DJs were talking so fast on air during the announcement breaks! We were all laughing so hard. It was truly one of the highlights of my time at Wright State, and a time I will never forget.

One thing about Wright State at that time. It was basically a commuter college. At the time, they only had one dorm, and it was mostly used for the handicapped since Wright State was at the forefront of the research on paraplegic and quadriplegics with electronic muscle stimulation. My parents were being transferred to Indianapolis, Indiana, but we knew I couldn't stay with them in Bellbrook, even if they weren't being transferred. They had looked at one-bedroom apartments, but they were expensive and had large deposits for college students.

Due to all this, my parents decided to purchase me a small older home in Dayton. It was about 1200 square feet with 4 bedrooms and 1 bathroom. The master bedroom, bathroom, and one bedroom were down, with the two remaining bedrooms up. Two very cute rooms with dormer windows. Unfortunately, they had gas wall heaters that didn't even work. My parents had to take those out and put in electric baseboard heaters. They also let me pick out some pretty floral wallpaper for the room that was my bedroom. I put some pretty mauve shears on the window, and it made such a cute, vintage-looking room. The other upstairs room was more of a sitting room and extra storage. I took both of the bedrooms upstairs once this was completed. Downstairs was the master and one guest bedroom, an eat-in kitchen with a washer and dryer in the kitchen. There was a small family room at the front of the house. It was older, so it didn't have central heat and air, just boiler heat and window unit air conditioning. Normally this was okay, it worked out unless it got really cold in the winter or really hot in the summer. I was able to rent out the master bedroom, which gave me a lot of the money I needed for the month. Now to find a roommate.

When I first started at the radio station, I met a girl looking for a place to move to. By now future roommate, Lisa, arranged to move in on the first of the next month. Then the Monday before she was going to move in the next weekend, Lisa came up to me and asked me if she could move in early. We sat and talked as she confided in me that her mom was out of town on business and she had been sexually assaulted by her mom's boyfriend that weekend. She said she desperately needed to get out of the house and wanted to see if I would let her move in a week early. I, of course, said yes, and she moved in that night. She was the first of many in my life that would confide something like this in me. I guess I'm easy to talk to, or somehow, they knew I would understand better than others. As for this point in my life, I wasn't feeling as alone by having someone in my life that also had been sexually assaulted, even though we rarely talked about it. I just didn't realize how many others out there were like me yet.

Besides going to school, I was working part-time at a store called Gold Circle. It was like a Walmart or Target. I really liked my job. I sat at the entrance to the fitting rooms and monitored who took what in and made sure those same items came back out. Once an hour, I would go in and clean up the rooms. (Oh, the stories I could tell. It's amazing how disgusting some people are!) The fitting rooms were on the women's side of the aisle, but across the aisle from the men's department, so the fitting rooms were for both. Men to the left, women to the right. I also answered the switchboard, which was located at the fitting room's podium. The phone didn't ring often, but I had to transfer the calls or get on the PA system and page a department to answer the call. Honestly, I thought it was one of the best jobs one could have if you are going to work in retail.

It was while I was at work on this job that one of the odder things in my life happened to me, and that is saying a lot.

One night, while I was sitting at the fitting room podium but with no one in the fitting room, a young lady who looked a few years older than me came up to me and asked if I was Jayna. I said yes. I did have a name tag on, so I guessed she was just trying to pronounce my name correctly. (For some reason, even though my name is spelled phonetically, people still can't figure out how to say it.) If not that, then it could have been someone in the store sending her to me to ask me a question. When I said yes, she asked if I was Jayna Barton. Well, my last name wasn't on my name tag, so now I'm a bit curious and very confused. With what I'm sure was a very quizzical look on my face, I said yes, albeit a bit slow and confused sounding. She proceeded to tell me that she had gone to Bellbrook High School but graduated the year before my freshman year. The reason she sought me out was the fact that her best friend, who had been on the women's tennis team, had been sexually assaulted by the same person as me. I was so very confused and worried. I had no idea how she knew about it or about me, especially since it had not been made public. I'm sure my confusion showed on my face. She went on to say that her best friend had also been told the same line as me, "no physical proof, no witnesses, and nothing in his past to indicate such a thing".

I'm sure I looked somewhat like a deer in headlights by now, with my mouth gaping open. I didn't know what to say. I was completely speechless, and I started shaking. I grabbed the podium to steady myself. Obviously, they didn't put her friend's accusations in his records, which is why it wasn't there to protect others like myself. She didn't tell me her name, nor the name of her friend. For some reason, I didn't ask either. In fact, I didn't really say anything at all. I think I was just in such shock. It is possible she did tell me, and I was too much in shock to remember it. I was shaking and nauseous for the rest of my shift and so anxious to get out of there. I didn't want to say anything or alert a manager as I had not told anyone at the store about my history. I was still so confused about how she knew what happened to me, scared that if she knew, then others knew, and his attorneys would be coming after me. I was feeling so sick to my stomach. I needed to leave and wrap my head around what I had just learned. Luckily, I only had a little over an hour left of my shift, and the store was pretty quiet. To this day, I don't know who she was or how she knew.

The next few weeks were then, and still are, a blur to me. I'm not sure why since I normally have an excellent memory. I can only guess it's just my brain's way of protecting me. I know somehow, my mom had gotten in touch with a reporter from the *CB Times*, a small newspaper that served Centerville and Bellbrook as well as other small towns around the area. Mom and I met with her at her house a week or two later.

The reporter proceeded to tell us that, first of all, my police report wasn't lost. No police department was stupid enough that they would lose a report or destroy it. We just needed the right person to ask for it. She arranged to have our state representative's office request it. Guess what. Magically it appeared! (They claimed it had fallen behind a file cabinet.) Thinking about the girl who approached me at work and told me about it happening before me, I wanted to make sure that this could not happen again to someone else, or if it did, the school couldn't say "nothing in his past history to indicate such a thing". We may not have had the internet back then, but we did have newspapers, and they last forever too! The reporter also suggested we get an attorney to protect ourselves, as she helped us take up the fight to protect others. I did not set out to pick a fight nor set out on a mission to protect others. It just sorta happened. I don't even know how this ball started rolling. That being said, I'm so glad it did. I don't know if I did help anyone, but since I haven't heard about this happening again, I hope it did put an end to this nightmare.

One thing to remember, this is 1986 and unlike today, where reporters are actively looking for these types of police reports. Back then, things like this were rarely reported on or even talked about. I really felt it was important to get something out there to protect the next girl. I also hoped this would give the school a wake-up call and protect the students - not the staff! This was before the internet, so I needed something with a public record.

We chose the school board meeting. So, with the help of this reporter, we arrived at the school board meeting of my former school district armed with my parents, my boyfriend (for moral support), my attorney, my reporter, a reporter from the *Dayton Daily News*, and one of the local TV station's news teams. I was very nervous. All I said to the school board was that it was a faculty member, my senior year, and just the fact that I was locked in his van on school property. I didn't say what season, didn't say what kind of faculty member, didn't say what event, didn't say on which school property (remember, it wasn't the high school), and didn't even say what month it happened. Most of the coaches drove vans, so even that wasn't much of a clue. If you remember back, I was involved in something every season of every year in high school, so I kept it as vague as possible to avoid the threat of slander.

After I spoke at the meeting, the news interviewed me in the hallway, along with my attorney, so they could get a few more details. It was still not reported on like it is today, so they didn't ask for any of the sensitive details about what exactly happened. They did make sure any questions that were important were asked and answered. It aired on the local news the next night, and from what I heard, by the basketball game that night, everyone had figured out who it was.

I just wanted something on the record somewhere so that the next girl wouldn't be told: "there was nothing in his past to indicate such a thing". The school might not make a record of it. The police might not make a record of it. But now there was one in the press, and that doesn't ever go away. Plus, it was in the minutes of the school board meeting too. It wasn't much, but I hoped that either it would stop him from doing this again to another girl, or at least she would have some form of recourse if it did happen again. Plus, it made all the parents and students in the district more aware and, hopefully, more cautious. Most thought nothing like this could happen in our innocent hamlet of a town. I used to think the same thing - till reality taught me differently.

Despite how difficult it all was, I was proud of what I had done and hoped it worked to prevent or protect any future victims. Whether it did or not, I don't know and probably never will. But it was the right thing to do. I was starting to find my voice. This was my first real step to healing myself and an even bigger step into what would become my future of wanting to help others.

What I didn't realize at the time was just how much healing I still needed to do. `

This all didn't come without a cost, though. By now, I had left Gold Circle and was working as a waitress in a Mexican restaurant. Steve worked there with me, too, as a bookkeeper and host. The restaurant had a bar area in the next room, up a few steps. So when you entered the restaurant, you could go straight and stop at the podium and be seated for food, or turn left at the podium and go up the few stairs to the bar area.

One night, I was standing at the host podium where Steve was and checking when I had another table coming up. As I said, the podium is where people come down from the bar land before turning right to go out the door. As I was standing there chatting with Steve, one of the former band moms came down the stairs. Let's just say she had been drinking heavily. She looked at me and said, "How dare you!". I just looked at her blankly and said, "What?" Then she proceeded to say, very loudly to me, "How dare you! How dare you accuse someone with such a gleaming white reputation of something so horrific?"

Steve, at this point, left to get a manager. I stayed as calm as possible. Knowing she was drunk and I had the truth on my side helped me stay calm, and just responded with a simple, "Who are you talking about?" Getting louder, she says, "You know damn well who I am talking about! I know you are accusing (insert the correct name here)." I took a deep breath and just calmly said, "I know who I am talking about, but I have never actually said who it is. If you think it's a particular person, then how can you say that person has such a gleaming white reputation?" It looked like she was just about to haul off and hit me at that point, but my manager stopped her and escorted her out the door.

First, while arguing with a drunk person may be fun, it's a losing battle. I had to step to the back and regain my composure after this little confrontation. The staff had put their arms around me and whisked me off to the kitchen to calm me down (and find out what was going on), and our manager offered to let me go home, but I said I was fine now that she was gone. I took a couple of minutes to regain my composure, screwed a smile on my face, and went to serve my customers.

Another thing that happened after all this came out was one day when Steve went to a TCBY Yogurt shop. He ran into one of our teachers (again, not going to mention who because it's not necessary at this point).

Now, this was a teacher that had to know something serious was wrong with me and the school. She taught in the classroom right across the hall from my attacker. Since the school didn't have air conditioning, the teachers would open their windows and teach with the doors open to create a cross breeze. Remember, for the first couple of weeks, while the school looked into the matter, my attacker wasn't allowed at school. Once he came back, the only concession the school would make was that he was not allowed in the hall at the same time as me. Well, since this teacher taught right across the hall, I had to listen to my attacker teach every single day - twice a day, in fact, as I had this teacher for two different classes. Now, I had gone from someone who was an overachiever that made 4 projects when everyone else only did one since I had extra time. My grades had fallen from A's to D's in the two classes. Once my attacker was back and impacting my mental health every single day, I stopped doing anything else in class as all the assigned work was done.

Anyway, Steve ran into this teacher at TCBY, and she asked Steve if he still hung out with me. He said yes. Then she asked if I was still crazy. When he saw me next, he hesitated to tell me because he was afraid of upsetting me, but really felt I should know. This is what I was subjected to. Half the teachers and staff sided with me, being disgusted with a school that didn't care about protecting its students (some even quit over it once they found out), and the other half that called me crazy or a liar. I would love to say I didn't care what they thought, as they were no longer a part of my life, but that would be a lie. I really didn't understand how the people who should have protected me would rather just tear me down. Did that somehow make them feel better to believe this was a lie rather than face the fact that a fellow teacher could do something like this or because they realized they failed to protect their students? I will never know or understand.

As an adult looking back on the situation, I can see just how wrong what she said was. No teacher should ever disparage a student to another student. It doesn't matter whether they are still in school or not, and it doesn't matter what it is about. That is just NOT appropriate at any time for any reason.

While I know everything I did was a good thing, that whole process, the backlash after, as well as my work, was taking a toll on my grades and my mental health. I was on academic warning when I registered for classes again. Before I could complete my third quarter, I dropped out. It was now spring of 1987, and I was only 19 years old, but life had definitely gotten in the way of school.

It had also gotten in the way of spending time with my best friend from high school, whose cancer had sadly progressed as well. She was now fully bedridden. When I would visit, she didn't even know who I was half the time, and even if she knew me, she would talk about things that never happened. It was so sad. She was only 20 years old. I felt so guilty and truly felt like I was such a horrible friend for not going out to see her more. She deserved more of my time, love, and support, but I just didn't have any more time or energy left to give. I wasn't even giving myself the time needed to heal. My self-esteem was still extremely low, and I had not gotten into any counseling yet for the assault.

I dropped out of that term thinking I would regroup and get my head on straight again and then continue my schooling. Being the strong person that I thought I was, I figured I could just regroup on my own and get my head in a better place. Boy, was I wrong.

During this same time, I was involved with something fun and interesting. That thing is The Rocky Horror Picture Show. One Saturday night after work at the Mexican restaurant, he suggested we go to Rocky Horror at midnight. I didn't know what Rocky Horror was, but I was game for just about anything. I was very tired, though. So we went, and I still couldn't tell you much about it as I fell asleep pretty early into the show.

Don't know what Rocky Horror is? Well, it's basically a B movie from 1975. Somehow it developed a cult following, and it became a whole thing. I call it a show because the movie is playing on the screen, but we would bring the film to life in the theater while it was showing on the screen. We created our own cast that played each of the characters week after week. Slowly we would create a similar costume to the movie. We would then act out throughout the theater. That's just the beginning, though. Several of the scenes have audience participation. For example, towards the beginning of the film, Brad and Janet are going to a wedding. They get caught in the rice throwing, so the audience, who brought their own rice, would throw it at us as we ran down the aisle of the theater. There were times when the audience would throw playing cards, stand up and dance the Time Warp with us, and all kinds of things.

This is how I met Amy. Steve and I started going every week. The second week I even stayed awake! Eventually, I started asking the cast how I could get involved. They basically shut me out. Since people ask them that every week I wasn't upset about it. I would go in and talk to the girls as they were getting their costumes and makeup on to get to know them, though.

One day, they asked if I still wanted to get involved. Their Columbia wasn't going to be there that week and wanted to know if I wanted to sub in. YES! Well, I can say that I sucked. I got to know the cast, and we were asked to join them at Denny's after we cleaned up the theater. Oh, I forgot to mention, we got in free because we had to clean the theater after it was over. That would take about 30 minutes. One guy brought a leaf blower each week and would just blow everything to the front, and we would take big shovels and trash cans to clean all that up, then a quick vacuum to finish it off. After the theater was clean, we all would head to Denny's and hang out for a couple of hours, having a VERY early breakfast (we would arrive about 2:30 am).

I started hanging out with the cast during the week. Of course, we would watch a wonky copy of the movie that one guy recorded the one and only time it was shown on tv. We watched over and over. I also got the cassette of the soundtrack, so I could truly learn the songs. Eventually, I joined the cast full-time as Magenta, then got promoted to Janet (who was very much like me). These new friends became so important in my life.

Chapter 3

Potholes and Detours

When summer came around, I thought I had gotten things back in order and had my head screwed on straight. Well, that's what I thought at the time anyway. Instead of going back to Wright State, though, I registered at Sinclair Community College. There were just too many former Bellbrook students at Wright State, and I needed a change. Since things have come out, I now felt like all of them were staring at me all the time. I'm sure that was just in my head but still was a problem.

I liked Sinclair enough. I even tried out to be a cheerleader, but still not being in a good place mentally, I dropped out before the tryouts finished. I found out later I was one of the top choices and would have made it. Still have a small regret that I didn't finish the tryouts, but my head just wasn't in the right place. I just dipped my toe into the water at first by taking one class, Accounting, the first summer. In the fall, I added more business classes, and for fun and my fitness credit, I took bowling. You have to appreciate a college with its own bowling alley!

This is also where I made a couple of new and amazing friends. The first became one of my dearest friends ever. His name was Sam, and he was my bowling partner in class. I had a little extra fun in class because I made bowling shirts with our team's name (the Spare Ribs) just for chuckles and giggles. Sam loved it! The instructor was more serious and not very impressed with the shirts. That's okay. We were still having fun.

He also loved to shop, and that was great with me too. Shopping has always been one of my favorite past times. Though I basically won't pay full price for anything. I am the queen of discounts. Sam was always smiling and happy, and up for anything. This was probably due to the medications that he took, as he had had a brain tumor since he was younger. He was always happy, though, with a great outlook on life, and that is what is most important. Since he almost died at 12 years old, he looked at each and every day as a gift. It was so nice to be around someone who always brought joy and laughter wherever he went. I needed that in my life. I'm pretty sure he had a crush on me, but I also knew he wouldn't date me or anyone else. He always said he wouldn't put anyone through that because of his tumor. I respect that and kept things just as best friends. We saw each other practically every day.

I also met Valerie. She and her husband would come to the bowling alley to do homework. I'm not sure how a bowling alley is a good place to study, but whatever works for them! Imagine a bowling alley with 12 lanes, all being used by a class, with the professor yelling from lane to lane and jumping up to show someone how something is done. The loud crashing sounds of pins being hit and falling along with the rolling sound of the balls being returned echoed around the whole space. There was also music playing in the background.

Somehow, they found this to be a great place to study. I guess whatever works for someone.

Valerie was a mom and going back to school with an elementary-age son. She was so very sweet and kind. At one point, she, too, opened up to me. She had been raped at knifepoint at a very young age (12, I think) while walking home from school. This caused her a lot of trauma, which she was trying to work through. We, Valerie, her husband, Sam, and myself, would all play cards at the bowling alley before Sam and I's class. Every week they tried harder and harder to get me to understand Euchre, but it never worked. I still can't play that game to this day. It was wonderful, though. I will always treasure those times. Her husband, at first, was nice enough, but my opinions of him quickly changed. More on that later, but I'm 100% sure he is why Valerie and I lost touch, but again, that's a story for another time.

Wait, I'm getting ahead of myself. Let's go back to the summer. Back when my roommate, Lisa, was still living with me, she would hear me walking around at night in my room and sometimes would hear me talking. While I don't think I ever sleepwalked before this time, I did talk in my sleep. She was worried, though. In fact, several of my friends were. I needed to try and get in a better place mentally.

Once I started hanging out with Amy, she let me know that she had been raped multiple times. Once a stranger rape, the other two were date rapes. Amy was worried about me like others were, and she suggested a counselor that she had seen too, and also a psychiatrist in the same group. The psychiatrist diagnosed me with night terrors and put me on one of the early anti-depressants for a couple of months, and the counselor got me talking. My counselor, Paul, was amazing. I give him a lot of the credit for me being able to get back to a halfway decent place and start back to school at Sinclair. He not only worked with me on my assault issues but also on my self-esteem issues.

Let me say to everyone reading this story, don't be afraid of reaching out for help. Counseling is so beneficial. No one will judge you for it, and you need to do what is best for you. Now, you may need to try out a couple of therapists before you find the right match, and that's okay. It's just part of the process. I lucked out by having a personal recommendation, and I had a great counselor without having to search.

Right before I started at Sinclair, I was having my final session with Paul. He said one thing that was so profound and stuck with me... and I'm so glad it did. At my last session, he asked me, "What are you going to do when this happens again?". Notice he didn't say "IF it happens". He said "WHEN it happens" again. Remember back when I started at Wright State, my roommate was assaulted by her mom's boyfriend, and the girl, Amy, that recommended I see Paul, had been date raped multiple times over the years, and Valerie had been a rape victim as a child. Not to mention I knew about the girl that was supposedly assaulted by my attacker five years before me. None of us had met through any sort of group or anything, these are just the women placed in my life. Though I was still healing, this one question really stuck with me. He didn't want me to answer that question right away, he just wanted me to think about it. And think about it, I did - a lot. Of all the good he did for me, he had no idea how much of an impact this one question would have on my life. I wish I had stayed in touch with him so I could tell him thank you.

As I was wrapping up classes for the fall at Sinclair, life threw another pothole into my life.

Let me pause for a moment and tell you about my family. On my dad's side, there was only my dad and me. His stepfather was also in my life a bit. He joined our family when I was three years old. My dad's younger brother, Jeff, had passed away at only like 28 years old when I was in 3rd grade, and his mom, my grandma, passed when I was 12. Grandpa Ben, my dad's stepdad, had remarried but still considered my dad and I family.

On my mom's side, I had both grandparents, aunts and uncles, cousins, and extended family. One problem, though, they were all in Missouri and Arkansas.... I had moved around a LOT growing up. I would get to see my mom's family for a week each summer and on several Christmases. As a whole, I wasn't close to many of them at that time because I just didn't really know them. My cousin Timmy was the exception. He and I were the two youngest. For holiday dinners, we were the two eating on TV trays in the family room. From what I've been told and seen pictures of, I played with him more when I was very little when we were living in the St. Louis area and could come down easier to visit. In fact, many people thought he and I were twins. When we would go to the mall with my aunt, mom, and grandma, people would ask whose twins we were. Tim didn't get upset that I was being called his sister, only that they couldn't see that he was older! Well, he was 15 months older, so I'll give him that one.

One of the first memories I have of Tim was when I was like 4, and he was 5. We were in his backyard, and he was trying to teach me to play catch. On one of the first throws, the ball hit my glove, then bounced up and hit me in the face. It wasn't even hard enough to make my lip or nose bleed, but I was always a wimp. I ran into the house crying. Timmy also ran into the house crying. While my mom was trying to calm me down, he ripped the covers off a couple of his coloring books and wrote "I'm sorry" notes to me. I still have those covers to this day. (A picture of one of the covers will be in the photo album at the end of this book.)

When going to Missouri, he was always the person I was most excited to see. I always wanted to know when we would get to see Timmy and his big brother Kelly. Over the years, they would take me to movies and to high school basketball games. Tim would ride bikes with me and teach me to play Rock 'Em, Sock 'Em Robots, and electronic football. I was very close to him. (Not sure he felt the same way, but that's ok.)

In November 1987, I hit that next pothole life gave me. Tim committed suicide at only 20 years old. I was absolutely devastated. As someone that had struggled with depression most of my life, the thoughts of suicide had entered my mind more than once. I probably had a better understanding than most in my family of what that level of depression does to your mindset. That being said, I just wished he had reached out to someone. He had so many people in his circle, and any or all of them would have helped. This created a new level of pain and confusion in my life. My mom did not want me to go to the funeral and refused to take me with them, so I had no choice but to stay back in Ohio. I hated this! I didn't get to say a proper goodbye. I hope he knows just how much he is missed every day by me and so many others whose lives he touched.

The one and only positive that came out of this was that I never thought about suicide again. Being the one left behind is not what anyone thinks about when in that level of depression, and that's what allows you to have those kinds of thoughts. Now that I had been the one left behind, I could no longer push those thoughts out of my mind; therefore, never seriously thought about suicide again. I just wish I could have figured this out some other way.

The day I found out was a bad day for more reasons than just Tim's suicide, though. Now back to something I eluded to earlier. My thoughts about Valerie's husband. I had called Valerie earlier in the day to let her know that Timmy died. She obviously told her husband, which is fine and expected. On his way home late that night, he stopped by my house. It was late enough that I had already gone to bed, but when I saw it was him, I let him in.

I was glad, at first, that my friends were concerned enough to be checking on me. Because I had been in bed, I was only in my nightshirt. Even though he was sitting across the room from me, I was getting some really creepy vibes from him. I curled up in my Papasan chair and tried pulling my nightshirt over my knees to cover myself more. I tried to tell him I didn't need company and just needed sleep, but he didn't take the hint and wouldn't leave. I kept myself curled up in my Papasan chair. I'm not sure how long he was there; probably at least an hour or more before he finally left. I was so thankful when he left. I even watched through the blinds to make sure that he really was leaving. I didn't know why I was feeling like this. I brushed it off at the time, thinking I was just getting weird vibes because of the grief. It really bothered me, though.

He was already making me suspicious because he would say

Valerie had a breakdown and was in the hospital and couldn't have visitors. This would go on to happen 3-4 times a year. Now I was wondering if he wasn't the guy I thought he was and was doing something to hurt her or at the very least, purposely keeping her from her friends and family. Was it really a breakdown or did she possibly have cuts or bruises that would give him away? This thought now kept me up all that night. She would never say anything. The only time she ever said something to me was one day for my photography class, I was doing portraits, so I did her hair and makeup since it was a black-and-white photo shoot. Makeup is really different for those. I guess when she got home, he threw a fit about the makeup - and the hair! She said he was so mad he hit the wall with his fists.

I'll never know what happened to her as one day, a couple of years later, all communication just ended. I had a letter that just was marked "no longer at this address". There were a couple more things that happened later on that year that at least justified the creepy vibes that night, like him trying to make a pass at me and shut me in a room with him at my going away party, and that just makes me wonder more whatever happened to her and what part he played in it. Wish I knew more about that story and what happened after I left. I wasn't there to protect her anymore, and that scares me. But I'm getting ahead of myself again.

I have to admit, by this point in life, I was getting pretty numb to everything. The easiest way not to deal with my feelings was to repress them. Well, I got VERY good at that. I wasn't looking for much when school started. When I tried out for cheerleading, I had lost my competitive edge, my spirit, and my joy. Not good traits for a cheerleader.

The bowling class in the fall and my friendship with Sam did so much to bring fun and laughter back into my life, though, at least when we were hanging out together. He was so awesome! We would travel to Cincinnati to go outlet shopping, we bought our own bowling balls, we would go ice skating or to movies, or whatever came to our minds. He also loved my home fries! Sam knew that I hated peeling the potatoes but never minded the hour it took to cook them properly. He would offer to peel the potatoes if I would make them, even if it was already midnight when he asked. I could never tell him no, so we had a lot of late-night home fries. I still remember vividly Sam sitting on my dryer next to the stove while I cooked the home fries. We would just laugh and laugh. Sam was so special. Even his family was wonderful and just welcomed me in. He was the ray of sunshine I truly needed in my life.

During this time, I also met Pat. Well, I had actually met him when I was in high school as he worked for a friend of mine's dad at a camera store. I honestly didn't really remember him, but he remembered me. I was told Pat had a crush on me back when I was in high school visiting the camera store, but Brad was usually the one I worked with. I had run across Brad one day when I was in college, and he re-introduced me to Pat. We hadn't dated very long when he proposed to me. For those who needed to catch up on my timeline, at this point, I was only 19 but soon to be 20. Right after I turned 20, though, life threw a detour at me.

One day, fairly early in the day, my friend Steve showed up at my door. He was visibly upset and pacing around. He said he had received a call from Kim's sister. He had been in the shower, so she had left a message on the answering machine for him to call her. He just couldn't do it. He knew in his heart why she was calling. So, I picked up the phone and called her to confirm what we both already knew, that Kim had passed away.

First, I comforted Steve. This was the first death of someone close to him, and even though we knew this day would come, he wasn't taking it well. I was just back to being numb. Besides, I had to be strong to help Steve, who was very sad and upset. Sadly, by this point, deaths and funerals are not unusual to me anymore. After I got Steve composed, we headed out to Kim's sister's house.

I felt sad for the family, but I did not show much emotion. In fact, I think they got mad at me because I was not crying or visibly sad. They were also upset I hadn't come out to see her much lately. Her family took my being numb as not caring. Let me say to everyone that grief is shown in many different ways. Never hold it against anyone over how they do or do not show emotions in times of stress or sorrow. You never know what they are actually feeling on the inside or how they are grieving in private. And never feel guilty yourself for the way you do or do not express your emotions. They are yours and yours alone. That being said, I've gotten to where I kinda go into crisis mode, and instead of showing my emotions, I suppress them so I can help everyone else navigate the situation at hand, as I had done with Kim's death.

Actually, I was feeling more guilt than sadness. The last few times I had visited Kim, she didn't even know where she was and didn't even recognize those around her. She wasn't Kim anymore. People are mad at me for saying or even thinking that, but that was reality. I did feel tremendous guilt, though. If I had been a better friend, I would have gone out and visited more and been there for her and her family. I wasn't trying to be selfish or ignore her. I was just trying to keep my head above water as it was and not even doing a great job of that. Outside of Steve, no one there knew what all I had been dealing with since high school. I had never shared any of it with her family. Most people I only told tiny bits and pieces to because I didn't want to appear weak and was still in constant fear of the teacher's attorneys coming after me. I will never hold anything against her family because I had not shared any of that with them. But I was, at that moment, wishing things were different and that I had been there more for her and her family. That is one regret I will have for the rest of my life.

A few weeks later, I took the day off to run errands and mail my wedding invitations. After going to the post office, I stopped at the Dayton Mall. It had been a sunny day when I arrived, but while there, a brief but very heavy rainstorm hit as I was about to leave. I was waiting in that space between the outside and inside doors of one of the department stores with an older woman and a middle-aged man. It had been raining heavily for over 5 minutes and not showing any signs of it letting up. The kind of rain that is a sheet that you can't hardly see through.

I had no idea how long this rain would last. When I thought it was letting up a bit (but still very heavy rain), I decided to chance it and run to my car. I got in and slammed the door, and started the car as I was very wet and needed my heater to dry me off. I then turned to the passenger seat to put my bags down, as they were wrapped around my wrists so I wouldn't drop them while running in the rain. All of a sudden my car door opened again. It was the man waiting in the entry area with me. Startled and thinking it was someone who needed help or directions or something, I just stared for a second as I was being shoved over to the passenger seat while the man jumped in my car with a gun. When I hit the passenger door, I remember being mad at the door because it was locked and, therefore, I had no way to exit. The man took off driving as I started crying and basically hyperventilating. I completely lost it. This was the absolute worst thing I could do! I was losing the ability to fight or be vigilant about where I was or whatever else I would need to survive. All I could think of was that I was going to disappear, and my family would be looking at my picture on a milk carton soon.

Crisis mode finally kicked in, and I regained my composure enough that I could start assessing the situation. I knew I was in BIG trouble. We were driving through a very rural area not far from the mall, but where there was no traffic and houses were several acres apart. A .25 caliber gun was being held to the back of my neck, right on the spinal cord. A shot probably wouldn't kill me, but would probably paralyze me. I think this thought scared me more than death did. This is when my angels came back to help me out once again.

The perpetrator was asking me questions, which I was trying to answer, but not in a way that I was giving him too much information so he would not be able to find me again if I got out of this, but also wanted to seem cooperative so he would not get mad and shoot me. As before, I'm not going into all the gory details, as it's not necessary, and I don't want to trigger anyone reading this. As I just stated, the area behind the mall at that time was very rural and wooded, which is where he was driving me around at. After he finished raping me, he drove me back to the mall. By this time, the rain had let up quite a bit, and I could see and recognize where I was.

Back in high school, Steve and I had season passes to Kings Island. We would take the back way to get there through these little towns and back roads. We were now on these same back roads. I slipped up and let on that I knew where we were. Stupid move! My angels forgot to grab my tongue on that one! Not much later, the guy apologized to me for having to do this to me. Luckily, my angels were back and held back my tongue as all I wanted to do was say something snarky and tell this person off, as by now, he no longer had the gun at my neck. My angels did a great job watching over me, though, and got me back to the mall safely.

I went straight to my future husband and father-in-law's workplace (they worked at the same place), as they worked fairly close to the mall. I was barely holding it together. Luckily, I had not had to speak yet. Cheryl, the receptionist, kept asking me what was wrong, and I just shook my head. I'm sure I looked like a drowned rat with my hair now mostly dry but tangled from him holding my hair when it was wet and my clothes all wet and disheveled. She then asked if I had been in a car accident. I again shook my head no. She had paged Pat, and being concerned, she asked once again what was wrong. I just said, "I was raped." As soon as the words left my mouth as to the reality of what happened, that single sentence brought me to my knees, and I collapsed on the floor, crying uncontrollably. This was a total breakdown.

Cheryl ripped off her headset, tossing it onto her desk as she bolted for the warehouse where Pat worked. Everyone in the office knew me, so when they saw me like that through the open door to the offices, they immediately took me to the board room while Cheryl was getting Pat. They hadn't heard what I had said to Cheryl, so they were whispering among themselves and trying to get me to talk. I just couldn't. Words just would not come out. I guess Cheryl had told them what I said. At first, I didn't even want to go to the police station as I was afraid my attacker would track me down if I did. He had looked at my driver's license while he still had me at gunpoint and threatened me if I went to the police. I did eventually allow Pat and his dad to take me to the police station. They all looked after me until they could get the car brought to the door and get me to the police station. Unfortunately, this included someone getting me coffee to calm me down. I say, unfortunately, because that likely destroyed some of the evidence. Their hearts were in the right place, plus they didn't know at that point what had happened, so they just didn't know that was damaging. Cheryl filled them in after I left, from what I heard.

While waiting for the detective, Pat was running his fingers through my hair and was trying to break it up. I swatted his hand away. I didn't mean to be mean about it, but that was evidence, and I knew it. After I filed my police report and was heavily questioned by the police, I went to the hospital and went through the hell of a rape kit. Don't get me wrong, I'm glad I did it so he could be prosecuted, but a rape kit is humiliating. They also had to cut chunks of my hair out that were stuck together by the evidence that was on it. They took my clothes as evidence too. Then they gave me some sort of shot, and I was then sat in the waiting room while they finished processing the rape kit. I was just in a hospital gown and donated sweatpants. No bra or anything, as they took it all. It was so embarrassing. Again, I felt everyone was staring at me and felt so very exposed, especially since the hospital gown was white, and I no longer had my bra. When I got home, I went straight to bed. I didn't want to talk at all.

I had called my parents from the waiting room at the hospital. Mom answered, but dad was at a business dinner. Dad drove home so fast from the dinner that he doesn't even remember if he saw any stoplights, much less if they were red or green! My parents were living over in Indiana at this time, so they got over as soon as they could, but I didn't see them till the next day. When they arrived, I could hear everyone talking in the living room, but I was not emotionally able to be part of the conversation yet. I just stayed in bed, curled up with a big teddy bear. At this point, I don't remember feeling anything at all, not even a numb feeling. There really is no way to accurately describe the almost out-of-body experience I was having. I felt like my body and my soul were not in sync. I would reach up and feel where they cut the chunks out of my hair and would just cry.

Needless to say, now I was fully shattered into a thousand pieces. My boss was great and let me take off all the time I needed. This was good as the store I worked at was the opposite corner from the mall, and I could see the mall out the front windows, where our registers were at. About two weeks later, I went back to work, and Bob, my manager, stayed with me and said I didn't need to be there if I didn't want to. He could see I was trembling even though I was keeping my hands in the pockets of my apron to try and hide it. I told him I needed to be there. I can't hide forever and have to get my life back in order. He did tell me not to get on a register yet and just had me make new end-cap designs, as he knew I really liked doing that. Bob was such a great manager!

I wasn't able to go to classes either since I was afraid to park in the parking garage. Going anywhere at this point was a struggle. It was too late to withdraw from classes but could take an "I" (incomplete) in my classes and then take them again the next semester. The exception was my photography professor, who gave me an A. I thought it was a mistake because I hadn't completed half the assignments or taken the final exam. I called him when I got my grade report thinking he must have switched my grade with someone else. He said he thought I was too talented for B&W 1, and he wanted me in Color 1. Since B&W 1 was a prerequisite, he passed me. I had also told him why I wasn't attending classes, and he was gracious and said he would be happy to walk me in and out of the garage if I wanted, even if I wasn't going to his class. He tried to assure me that I would always be safe on campus. Well, I had thought that of a mall with lots of people in the middle of the day on a weekday too.

Let me say that, at this point, I needed therapy again! Pat needed therapy, and we needed couples' therapy too. This is a lot for any relationship to handle, especially one so young. That being said, we had no therapy at all. I had virtually no pride or self-esteem left. With what little misguided pride I had remaining, I said I still wanted to get married. Everyone tried to tell us to wait. The problem was that I didn't want people to think that some stranger had beaten me or, in some way, had some control over my life, so I continued full steam ahead. Big big big mistake! That was my misguided pride talking. The reality was that a stranger DID have control over my life. I just refused to see it or deal with it.

The other reality was I just didn't want to be getting married. I just didn't want people to think that I was weak or that some stranger had beaten me, and I didn't want to explain what happened to those that didn't already know.

I really hate to admit this, but in my mind, I turned the wedding into a play. We had a stage, set, script, costumes, music, etc. In fact, this was a major production. We had an opera singer, a recordist, and the handbell choir! It was a beautiful Lutheran church with candles on every other pew and a pulpit area that was in the center. My gown had been a sample, so it was a beautiful bridal satin gown with a chapel-length train and a cathedral-length veil. I looked like a princess. Even with that, I really didn't want this.

I had two wonderful guys in my life from my rifle team growing up. These two were my everything... my friends, brothers, and confidants, and would do just about anything for me. I know if I asked, they would have kidnapped me and taken the heat for me not getting married. I remember staring at the door to my dressing room, hoping against hope that the two of them would step in and take me away. (Not sure how they would have gotten me in the back of Jerry's Trans Am with the amount of dress I was wearing, but they would have found a way!)

Here's where it started to get weird for me. Yes, it's amazing that I can still claim something is weird in my life. After the bridesmaids had walked down the aisle and they had re-closed the doors where my dad and I were now waiting to walk down the aisle, those two guys showed up. I remember Rob looking at me and giving me a thumbs-up. They were too late! Sadly, as the ceremony was ending and we turn around for the priest to pronounce us husband and wife, I'm scanning the guests looking for them. But neither of them was there. After the photos were taken, we headed to the reception. There was a gift on the front of the gift table from them, but I didn't see them anywhere. Even after going from table to table, they weren't there.

I honestly was beginning to wonder if I just wanted them there so badly that I just imagined them showing up. Luckily, I asked my dad sometime later, and he confirmed they were at the wedding. I also asked Rob before I moved if they were there, and he said yes. He couldn't believe I didn't know why they didn't stay. I finally got him to admit that Jerry just couldn't watch me get married. He still had a crush on me even though we had not gone out since middle school. (Unless you count one date in college, but I was sure his car would come before me, so I didn't go on a second date.) UGH!

I would love to be able to apologize to Pat, as this marriage should never have taken place. I was broken with very raw emotions, and my fiancé turned husband didn't know how to handle me. How could he? He also did not have a chance to heal himself. At the time, I didn't realize how important that actually was. I'm not sure he knew either. As I am now older and I think wiser, I see how helpless he must have felt. How hurt he must have been watching me going through everything that night it happened. Plus, the anger he must have felt towards the person who did this to me. Maybe even confusion on why this was happening to him, and it was turning his life just as upside down as it was mine. This made him treat me like a china doll that could break in a single fall. This irritated me, but in hindsight, I actually was as fragile as a china doll, maybe even more fragile. Just six months after the wedding, I asked for a divorce.

I gave him no way to fix anything. I needed out of Ohio and every memory of it. It did not feel safe for me anymore. To make things even worse, I found out that I was not the only victim of what would later be labeled the Dayton Mall Rapist. I'm still mad that I didn't find out from the police. I found out from the radio. Radio alarms were the big thing back then. Imagine lying in bed, trying to ignore the early morning light flooding in from the windows as the music plays to gently wake you up. Then the news break comes on, and they announce another victim of the Dayton Mall Rapist. That will jolt you awake! It was even featured on Crime Stoppers, again without any warning to me, so I couldn't prepare myself. In the end, I was just the first of four victims, and a fifth escaped, which was how he got caught. In the research for this book, to make sure I had everything correct with dates and victims, I learned that there ended up being two different men, totally unrelated cases, that were considered the Dayton Mall Rapist in 1988. 4 of the 5 rapes were my attacker, the last one was determined to be another perpetrator. They didn't know that at the time, though. I'll put the articles about my attacker at the back of the book.

Not only did I no longer feel safe there, but I had no family left there. By now, my parents had moved to Texas, but I thought I needed to go back to Missouri and have a more laid-back life and get to know my extended family better. Find my roots, as it were. Besides, I had an image in my mind of Texas with 10-gallon hats, cowboy boots, and tumbleweeds everywhere. While it was hard to leave Steve, Sam, and Valerie, as they were friends so close that they were family to me, I needed to get out. I would never be able to heal in a place I don't feel safe while working or shopping or just trying to have fun with my friends. So, the day after the divorce was final, I moved.

I had just turned 21!

Chapter 4

Roadblock

When I left Ohio, it was a beautiful sunny day. One might even say the perfect spring day. Sam had come over to help me finish up and see me one last time. Mom had flown in from Texas a few days prior to help me move and make the drive to Missouri. Our 16-hour drive had great weather the whole way there as well. It was very sunny without too much wind or being overcast. We did know that it was supposed to rain in Springfield, so I was trying to beat the rain there. To make sure we made it sooner rather than later, we only made one or two stops along the way. Gas, food, and potty breaks all at one stop. This wasn't unusual for us, though. This is how we traveled to Missouri my whole life.

We got to my grandparent's house a little before 11:00 pm, unloaded the car, and just as I was bringing the very last item in, the sky opened up, and it began to pour. It didn't even sprinkle first. It was like the sky just opened up and began dumping water. Luckily, I was on the covered porch with the door open and going through it when the sky opened up. Whew! I just made it!

Now, my grandparents had the most amazing room darkening shades in every room of the house. When they are down, you don't see a thing. The next morning my mom comes in asking if I had looked outside yet. I was asleep, and I didn't even know it was morning yet as the room was so dark. I stand up, stumble to the window, and pull up the shade. I was blinded by the bright morning light reflecting off the snow. The 11 inches of snow! Well, this was certainly unexpected. I was supposed to meet my moving truck at the storage facility where I would store my stuff until I could get a place on my own again. The moving company didn't expect it either and had turned off their rig, and their engine froze up. A few hours later, they were able to get the rig fixed and get to the storage facility that afternoon. We very carefully made it to the storage facility too. It was like winter had to get one last storm in before spring arrived. At least I didn't have to drive in it to get to Missouri.

I thought it was lucky that I made it there before the storm, but really this should have been my warning sign that things were not going to go as planned. I came to Missouri to get closer to family, to get back on my feet, to improve my career and finances, to make new friends, and to go back to college. My dream had always been to go to Southwest Missouri State University (now it's just called Missouri State University, but it will always be SMSU to me). When I was living in Ohio, that hadn't been possible because we could not afford to pay for me as an out-of-state student. Now it would be possible, or so I thought at least.

Sam was supposed to call me the next day to see how the trip was. Since long-distance calls were expensive back then, he didn't want my grandparents to have to pay for the call since I was staying with them. Weirdly, he didn't call, though. With all that went on that day, I didn't think a lot about it till after dinner. Still no call. I still thought he was maybe giving me time to settle in. The next day, still no call. Ok, now I'm getting worried. I couldn't imagine him not calling. Two more days pass, and still no call. I decided I needed to call him and find out what was going on. I wasn't thinking anything happening to him, just wondering if, since I moved if he was cutting contact with me.

When I called, his mom answered. The day I moved, Sam slipped into a coma later that day. His parents, one, didn't know how to get in touch with me, and two, didn't want to worry me. Luckily, they were about to leave to pick him up from the hospital and bring him home. I felt so guilty. Did him getting up early to visit one last time, and did the stress of me moving cause this? He always told me, no, but he would never have said yes to me in a million years. I knew I needed out of Ohio, but this was a high cost, and I wasn't even the one having to pay it. I would never do anything that would hurt him. Luckily, he recovered just fine, and we continued to call and write letters all the time.

Things in Missouri did start off well for me, aside from the health scare with Sam. I immediately set out to find a job. I put in a few applications, and I signed up for Job Corp. With Job Corp, I get help with my resume and interview training. They also paid me as I looked for work. Soon after, I got a job at a local car dealership as the body shop receptionist and made a couple of great new friends, Nancy and Greg. I met Greg first at Job Corps before I got the job, as I had sparked a lively debate that continued through our lunch period on the first day for us at Job Corp. He then introduced me to his friend Nancy. The three of us became the best of friends. We either saw each other or talked on the phone every single day. We did all the typical things people my age should do; we went to the movies or watched movies together at home, shopped, or just hung out together, etc. The normal life of a 21-year-old. It was so nice to be living a normal life for the first time in a long time.

Nancy and I got really close. We did so much together. Later, she would be the one I turned to whenever my boyfriend and I broke up (which happened over and over). We met in May of 1989, and she is still one of my dearest friends to this day.

I had also gone back to church to the same church that had been a part of my family for decades. My grandfather was a deacon there, and my mom grew up with the same pastor that was still there. Reverend Charles was the one to marry my parents, and he was the one to do my baby dedication. In the end, he was also the paster that buried each of my grandparents when the time came. As I was looking for family and stability, I thought this would be a great place to start.

When I had visited once with a friend back when I was still living in Ohio, my pastor said to me, "Jayna, don't you fall asleep in another one of my sermons. If you do, I'll have to make you a deacon because only deacons are allowed to sleep in my sermons." We all laughed, and he gave me a big bear hug. I considered him family as he had been so intertwined with my family. I found out that going back to this church may not have been the great choice I thought it would be. First thing, I had a talk with the pastor. Since he was a good friend of the family, I was sure my grandparents had said something to him about what I had gone through before I got there. Well, at least I hope they had. When meeting with Rev. Charles, he really didn't know what to say to me. While pastors are trained in counseling, I don't think he had ever spoken to anyone that had actually been raped or sexually assaulted before. You could tell he was visibly uncomfortable and struggling with what to say to me.

He also didn't know what to do with me. As far as Sunday School classes go, the college and career class was where I should have been placed due to my age, but none of the members in that class were divorced, so he didn't think I would fit in. Instead, he put me in Adult 5, which was the divorced Sunday School class. Everyone in that class was 35 years old and older, though. This meant that the people I hung out with, even outside of class, were 35 and up. Most people in that class already had kids, too. College and Career is where I needed to be. Ok, I did love the kids, and they loved me too. I was still a normal 21-year-old, though. While I should have been with my age group, being overly mature for my age and with my life experiences, I didn't really feel super out of place, but this still was not the best place for me, as you will see later. What I needed was to just be treated as a normal 21-year-old girl.

I lived with my grandparents till the beginning of the next month, when I was able to get an apartment on my own again. It wasn't anything fancy, but it was a little over 500sf with a living room, galley kitchen, dining area, and one bedroom and bath. It was on the second floor with a balcony that overlooked the back parking lot and the trees that tried to block the railroad tracks. I was starting to get my life together again. I felt happy and safe for the first time in a long time. I still loved going to my grandparent's house for lunch even after I moved back out, though.

My grandparents made lunch the big meal of the day and just snacked or had leftovers for dinner. That meant an entire table of food for just the three of us for lunch. Grandma would make things like venison, but with it would be home fries, green beans, corn, and biscuits. Oh, and don't let me forget the two pieces of bologna, one each for Duke and Bullet (their dogs). She would also have something sweet for dessert. Papa would cut up the two pieces of bologna and slowly give each a piece throughout the meal, so they didn't beg from anyone else. Then after lunch, I would sit and watch an episode of Perry Mason with them before heading back to work. These are some of the memories I will cherish for the rest of my life.

Sam also came out to visit me. I missed him, and I loved having his spirit and laughter around me. I loved showing him around the town. Since I was actually born in Springfield, I got to show him lots of things about where my mom grew up and where I was born. Life in Missouri is so different from life in Ohio. He wasn't used to the super-friendly nature of the Ozark, though. We would often go to a store, and someone would hold the door open for me, then say hello and have a good day to me. Sam would ask who that was. Well, I never knew the people. That's just how we are. We try to be friendly to everyone. Sam found it weird, but also really liked it. He also got along well with my friends. He and Greg were actually so much alike. Personally, I tried to use this to get him to come live here, but in my heart, I knew that wasn't possible. It was worth a try, though.

When it came to my job, though, I was just doing typical office work. I answered the phone, sent paperwork over to the cashier so the customers could pay and pick up their cars, and processed warranty claims and paperwork. Office work was something that I had done a lot in the past, but it was boring. My aunt was a nurse, and since I was kind of tired of office work, I wanted to try my hand at something new.

Only being 21, and with all I had been through, I was still trying to figure out who I was and what I wanted to be when I grew up. I applied for and got accepted into the nursing assistant program at one of the local hospitals. I did well in the training program. Part was book learning and practical skills like taking a patient's vitals and basic care of patient's needs. The other part was spending 2 weeks on a floor and learning hands-on. I graduated 4 weeks later with a 100% on my exam. When I told my patients on the floor I trained on, they were all so proud of me. Next, I started working the night shift on the orthopedics floor. It was a good full-time job with benefits, and I loved almost all of my patients. A few of my patients I still tell stories about to this day. This time had a big impact on my life.

When I left my job at the dealership, one of my co-workers, Mark, took the opportunity to ask me out. Besides working at the dealership, he had a show on the college radio station, and he was a bartender at a local jazz club. I began hanging out there and eventually got a job there as a cocktail waitress. Well, kinda had to become a waitress as I was in the club after hours, and liquor control came in. The owner said I was there because I was in training. When they left, he asked me if I had any training as a cocktail waitress. I said, "yes". I did have some experience from when I worked at the Mexican restaurant in Ohio. We had a bar area where I worked from time to time. He then asked if I wanted a job. Well, I didn't want him to get in trouble, so I agreed. Best decision ever! I loved it!

Since I worked the night shift at the hospital, I had time to work at the club too. Honestly, I made more in a couple of days as a cocktail waitress than full-time as a nursing assistant. I was good at what I did at the hospital, but it was emotionally draining and physically hard. The jazz club was fun and energetic. In fact, I think the jazz club was actually one of my favorite jobs of all time. I was very good at it too. I had the worst section. The one that filled last and cleared first. It only had six tables, all designed for 6 people each, so not the date section. I still manage to out-tip both the other waitresses, though. It helped that I had regulars that would tip me just for my outfits, even if I didn't serve them a single drink that night. (I was a size 0 and loved to wear short skirts! Yes, I did it on purpose too.)

Mark and I never wanted customers to know we were dating. It would have affected both of our tips. The regulars were the only ones that knew I was dating one of the bartenders, and they weren't really happy about it. They always thought I could do better. Well, I'm sure some of them thought they were the better choice, but they didn't exactly say that. I still remember one night when Pete was sitting at the bar, and I was waiting for my order. He waited till my boyfriend was within earshot and said, loud enough to make sure he heard, "Why is it that the best women in the world are all dating all the schmucks in the world?" You might have guessed Mark wasn't too happy when he heard that, but outside of the momentary look on his face, he didn't say a word.

As it turned out, one of the other cocktail waitresses happened to live in my apartment complex. We had talked several times, and she was very concerned about me. She, too, had been a victim of sexual assault in her past and had a wonderful counselor she wanted me to see. Not sure why, but I resisted at first. I had had such a good experience with Paul, but I still was hesitant.

She decided one day that I WAS going, so she called and made the appointment for me. I didn't have much of a choice, so I finally agreed to go. Ok, let me say that I will be forever grateful to her for forcing me to go. My counselor, Diane, worked with me on not only the rape and assault but my anger issues that had built up over my lifetime. Some days she even had me in the playroom, so I had things to throw or hit safely. The playroom is usually used for children's therapy and is a room with all kinds of dolls, puppets, soft balls, and soft bats, along with paper and crayons. All the stuff needed to get a child to share the scary stuff that they are in therapy for. I never took full advantage of that, though, because it felt so silly to me. But one of the best things she did was that she got me journaling, which led to me writing my poetry again. I found out that I work out a lot of my issues and internal conflicts in my poetry. In fact, I still do that to this day. One of the first questions she asked me during my very first session was, "Do you live day to day or crisis to crisis?". I looked at her blankly, and I asked her earnestly, "What's the difference?". That told her a lot about where I was at.

Diane also said I needed to spend more time with people my own age. My response was, "Why? They are so immature". By this point, I was so much more comfortable with the people in my Sunday School class than people in their young 20s. Diane said that was not healthy for someone my age. Greg and Nancy were the only exceptions, but neither were the crazy 20s type. Well, Greg had a weird side but was serious as he worked in news at a Christian radio station. (I can only imagine how crazy of a YouTube channel he would have had if it was available back then!) Nancy was a former preacher's kid. All three of us were pretty mature for our ages.

Starting the third session with Diane, she started me

working through a book that I will recommend to any woman with anger issues. It's called "The Dance of Anger". I'll put information about it in the back of this book. I have given out my copy and had to re-order one for myself multiple times over the years. I still refer back to that book, and I still use a lot of the tips and techniques both Diane and the book taught me to this day. I'm so glad she was there to help me put my life back together. I didn't know how truly messed up I was until I started getting more of my emotional health back in order. I had repressed so much of my emotions to protect myself. She was patient and seemed to know exactly what I needed to do to heal. I'm sure I was a bit of a problem for her. Also, since I worked nights, I would miss appointments due to oversleeping, but she didn't give up on me for it.

About this time, Steve also came out to visit me. I couldn't take off work, but since I worked nights, we would hang out together during the day, and he would go out at night to explore Springfield himself. He really liked Springfield. He really didn't like Ohio, especially because that was where his alcoholic father was. I thought for a bit I could convince him to move here, but no such luck. I was just glad to still have him in my life.

During this time, one of my co-workers at the hospital, Mindy, needed a place to stay, so I let her be my roommate. She was a nurse aide working the night shift like me but in the other orthopedics wing. Mindy was on 3North, and I was on 3South. I wasn't looking for a roommate, but it really did help me out financially. It also helped her financially, plus her boyfriend lived downstairs from me. That is normally a win/win situation. Because I just had a one-bedroom apartment but did have a hide-a-bed sofa, that is where she slept. Well, I admit that it did help me out for a while, but more on that in a bit.

So now that I was getting my life back in order, it was time to look at going to SMSU. I walked around the campus. I loved the energy on campus, the look of the classic university buildings (Wright State looked like office buildings), and the sights and sounds of students hanging out together. It's weird, but I just had a strong feeling, like this was where I belonged. I could not wait to be going to school here. I quickly made an appointment with an admissions counselor so I could see what I needed to do to transfer my credits here.

I had the advantage that, by working the night shift, I would be able to attend classes during the day and could study during the down times at work. Many of the nursing assistants on the night shift did that. Some were going to school to become nurses, and others were just going to school and working nights so they could go to classes and study at work. I was so excited that I thought I had it all planned out. I had taken the SAT back in high school, but of course, SMSU only took the ACT. So, I looked into when the next test would be administered and got registered for it. I wasn't worried about taking it but would need to study a bit. I was just starting to study for my ACT exam when once again, life had to throw up another roadblock. Actually, a couple of them!

The first thing that hit me was one day when I started my period a couple of weeks late. It was the heaviest period I had ever had. I would think it would stop, then it would start up the next day. This went on for over a month. Mark actually got mad at me for it! Finally, I went to the doctor to have it checked out. By this time, I had bled for so long that he suspected I had had a miscarriage, but it would have been in the first couple of weeks of pregnancy. Again, since I bled for so long, he also didn't feel a D&C was needed. Nature took care of itself.

A week later, Mark broke up with me. And to add insult to injury, he broke up with me for another woman that he had been cheating on me with! He actually told me all about her. I knew in my heart he had cheated on me in the past, as Greg had seen him leaving local bars with women when we were together, but I was at work. I also would occasionally see an unfamiliar car in the drive, but his car was usually gone, so I couldn't learn more. He had also warned me early in the relationship that he may cheat, as it was in his nature. I stupidly told myself that even if he picked up some random girl, it was me he was coming home to. I did have a key to his apartment but never used it when he didn't know I'd be there. In hindsight, I should have. (I always had a fantasy of walking in and catching him in the act and breaking up with him when it would make him feel the most guilty.)

This time was obviously different. In this case, the woman he told me about was someone whom I didn't think I could compete with. She was a paralegal, and he always wanted to be a lawyer. She also had a young son, and he didn't think he could have kids. How could I compete with all that?! Plus, the amount of hurt that he inflicted by confirming that he had been cheating on me was extreme. All I could do was sit there and cry as he told me the details. Even though I had suspected it, he had been lying to me and gaslighting me about it. Now, we had been in an on-again-off-again relationship for most of our time together, but these were cases where we were on, and he chose to cheat on me instead of breaking up with me.

That was until now. This time when he cheated, he then

broke up with me. This was just a few days after Christmas and a week after my doctor's visit. I was absolutely crushed. What a way to end the year. Plus, I didn't see how I was going to be able to move on here. I would have to give up working at the jazz club or would have to face seeing them being there together when he worked. He also lived in almost the center of town, so how to drive around and not drive past his place? The dealership we had worked at was across from the K-Mart, so again, I'd have to drive by there knowing he was there and not be able to see him. I thought my life was turned upside down all over again, and just when I thought it was finally getting back to normal.

If that wasn't enough, on January 1st, my roommate moved out. No warning. So, I had to come up with her share of the rent instantly. Since she wasn't on the lease, I was stuck for everything. I was very mad at her, and the timing couldn't have been worse because of quitting the jazz club where I made most of my money, but that wasn't even the worst of what she did. A week or two later, I got my phone bill. Remember, this is the late 1980s, so no cell phones and long-distance calls were expensive. When I got my phone bill, Mindy had racked up over $600 in long-distance calls to her mother in Minnesota! I couldn't pay that much, and my phone got disconnected. Now I was mad, hurt, and frustrated. That night I went to the radio station where my friend Greg worked at night. After we talked for a while, he asked me what I was going to do. I borrowed a line from the movies and said, "When God closes a door, he opens a window, and I'm going through the window. I'll call mom tomorrow and see about moving to Texas."

So that is exactly what I did. My parents had moved to Texas just before I had moved to Missouri. In fact, they had wanted me to move to Texas instead of Missouri originally.

Back then, I had an image of Texas in my head of tumbleweeds, cowboy boots, and hats, with everyone having a 6-shooter on their hip. I think I had watched a few too many westerns growing up. Because of this, I chose Missouri instead. I also wanted to get to know my family better, and they were in Missouri and Arkansas. I called my mom and asked if she still wanted me to move down there. Of course, she said yes. So, I started packing up my things, quit my job, and the next Tuesday, my parents arrived to move me to Texas.

A day or two before my parents arrived, Mark stopped by to bring a couple of things I had forgotten in his apartment. I still remember so vividly how he was just standing in the middle of my living room, wearing his trench coat all buttoned up with the belt tied, and looking around at all the boxes. He couldn't or wouldn't make eye contact with me. Instead, he just looked at the ground. Mark handed me the book, and I placed it on top of a box. Then he handed me a ceramic mask I had given him as a gift. I tossed it across the room into a trash box, and you heard it break. I stood there staring at him, emotionless, while he just stared at the box. I really think he thought I'd still be around, and if things did not work out with this new girl and he could just get back with me again. I hope he knew just how much he messed up, and maybe that is why he wouldn't look me in the eyes. I did not get upset or yell or anything while he was there. I was just numb, which is now how I handled any trauma in my life. I just stayed as cold and neutral as I could. I wouldn't give him the satisfaction of knowing just how much he had hurt me.

In the end, I think what bothered me most about moving was not going to the one college I had always wanted to go to and would never get a chance to go to again. In fact, that was probably going to be my last chance at college, ever.

Chapter 5

Speed Bumps

I packed up my apartment and on Tuesday, January 17th, 1990, my parents arrived to move me down to Texas. Once I got here, I really felt this was where I was supposed to be. Everything just seemed to fall into place so easily. I arrived on a Tuesday night and picked up Wednesday's small little local newspaper. I made some calls from the want ads and had two interviews lined up on Thursday. I was offered a job at a bank as a teller on Friday. I started the following Monday.

My parent's had great neighbors that were all the kind that came out into the front yards most nights just to socialize. In fact, it was one of those neighbors that let my parents borrow their Suburban to move me with so that we could tow a small U-Haul trailer. Another neighbor found out that my 22nd birthday was a couple of weeks away, so they brought over some tickets for the local high-end movie theater so I could enjoy my birthday. (I had never seen a movie theater where you had to take an escalator to the second floor to go to the individual theaters. This was because they were the first to have what we now call stadium seating. For me... this was fancy!) On my birthday, I arrived at work, and, even though I was new at the bank, there was a donut and a card signed by everyone waiting there for me. I was actually very happy. I felt so welcomed and appreciated there.

That's not to say there weren't a couple of little speed bumps along the way, though. Like when I got the subpoena. It had actually arrived at my grandparents' house the week I moved. My grandparents gave them my parent's address, but I guess there is a lot of paperwork to have me served in Texas instead. Only had about five to six weeks on my brand-new job, and now the State of Ohio was requesting my presence as a witness against the man who abducted and raped me. I basically had no warning. The trial was going to be the next week. Thanks, Ohio, for all the advance notice!

So, I was new on my job, and now I'm going to have to ask for time off for an unknown amount of time. Plus, I was going to have to explain that I'm one of the victims. Not exactly something you want to tell your brand-new boss. I'm not one who hides my past, but it's not exactly something that had come up yet. It's also kinda embarrassing when new on a job and they really don't know me yet. Luckily the bank president was cool and didn't ask for any details. Just asked me to keep them updated on when I would be back. More belief that I was in the right place, finally.

I was not looking forward to going back to Ohio, though. I have to admit that I was extremely nervous. First, I was barely 22 years old and never had any experience with a courtroom unless you count watching those old reruns of Perry Mason with my grandparents. That alone would make someone nervous, but the thought of facing the person that abducted me held me at gunpoint, and raped me was terrifying!

I knew I had to do it, though. I needed to do it for myself and for others. I needed closure personally, and I needed to have a part in ending his terror of other women. In fact, from what I was told, this hadn't been his first time doing this. His MO with us was almost exactly what he did and said back in the 70s. He was on parole from those rapes when he attacked us. Well, no one becomes a serial rapist right out of the gate, but in this case, he had a history of this in his past and had been jailed for it before, according to the detectives. My testimony could put an end to that. Knowing I need to do this doesn't make it any less scary, though. Plus, it's a lot of pressure to put on someone who is barely an adult. So, a week later, I boarded a plane back to Ohio.

The State of Ohio arranged for my flight and also for a police officer to pick me up at the airport and bring me to the courthouse. Just as a side note, do you have any idea how many people stare at you when you are picked up by a uniformed police officer at an airport? She met me at the gate, walked with me to baggage claim, picked up my bags for me, then took me to her marked car that was parked at the curb. You could see people watching and whispering. Everyone was staring at me, or at least it felt that way. At least I got to sit in the front seat of the squad car, instead of being placed in the back like I was being arrested! I can look back on that now and laugh, but it wasn't funny at the time. My self-esteem wasn't yet ready for the stares and silent judgments – even from strangers. I wanted to yell at everyone to just mind their own business.

What I found out on arrival, though, was that I was the only victim of the four victims subpoenaed that was going to testify. (The other victim, they suspected, was from the other Dayton Mall rapist.) They each had their own reasons for not testifying. We assume the defense was waiting to see if I actually got on the plane to come back for the trial. After the officer left to pick me up at the airport, the defense team pled it out. I assume this was to get a lighter sentence. When I arrived, the officer told me all this in the car.

Once I got to the courthouse, the prosecutor let me know that they thanked me for coming all that way. Since I was going to be staying with my friend Sam's family, they gave me the money they would have given me for a hotel and said I should take them out for a nice dinner. They also said since it was a Friday, I could stay the whole weekend, and they would book my return flight for Monday morning, so I could visit with my friends. I appreciated that so much. Then we waited in the room to see if the judge would accept the plea deal and what the final sentence would be. He ended up pleading guilty to three counts of rape and one attempted kidnapping. This included two counts of a felon in possession of a firearm. The firearms charges were three years each for a total of six years that had no parole and were to be served before the rest of his sentence began. For the rapes and attempted kidnapping, he got 15-85 years to be served consecutively, starting after the weapons charges. As of today, he is 78 years old and still in jail. The next time he will be eligible for parole is December 2024. At that time, he will be 80 years old, but something tells me he's still not getting out.

After I was done at the courthouse, Sam drove me around to try and visit some of my friends from college. It was a weird kind of sightseeing tour. We drove by my old house I had in college. We also tried to stop at the house of some friends, but sadly, the two of them weren't home, so we went to the Taco Bell, where we used to go on late-night food runs. You know, all the normal touristy sightseeing areas!

We did stop by Malone Camera, where Brad and Pat still worked. (Pat had gone back to work there after our divorce.) Brad was excited to see me and gave me a big hug. Then he took me back to see Pat. Ok, maybe I should have called first. Pat took one look at me, and he looked like a deer in headlights. Not the reaction, I thought. We had parted on such good terms and even talked from time to time on the phone. I had never truly said I was sorry before that. Not sure I fully did then, either. It wasn't till I was much older and wiser that I would come to understand what all he must have gone through himself. I was too young, too broken, too selfish, and too naive to know. From what I hear, he had a good life after I left and met a wonderful woman, so hopefully, he sees it as a good thing in the end.

I did take Sam's family out for dinner Friday night as well. They didn't want me to pay, but I insisted, saying it was actually the state of Ohio paying, so they finally agreed. They had always been so good to me. We went to Chi-Chi's Tex-Mex, which is kinda funny since I lived in Texas, and to me, this was kinda fake Tex-Mex, but that's where they choose, so I didn't say a thing. Besides, I was having too much fun to say anything. Chi-Chi's was always decorated with lots of flags and banners, piñatas, and Sombreros. Lots and lots of color everywhere! A mariachi band walked around playing. We laughed for hours while swapping stories and his parents telling embarrassing stories about Sam. I don't think I could have asked for a better end to that night.

Steve came by on Saturday, and we all hung out and even visited one other friend from high school, although anything associated with Bellbrook I was trying to avoid. I was always afraid of the inevitable questions that could come up. Since Dave graduated the year before me, he didn't know what I was like during the end of my senior year. I also avoided The Dayton Mall. I didn't even want to drive by it. I know it's just a place, and the mall itself didn't do anything to me, but I just couldn't go back there. I really gave it too much power over me for far too long. But, then again, leading up to this weekend had been so stressful while thinking I was going to have to testify, and the stress that came with that meant I was now only going to do fun things now that it was over. I had a good weekend and headed home on Monday and back to work on Tuesday. That would be the last time I stepped foot in Ohio for over 30 years!

Once back in Texas, I went back to work at the bank and got on with rebuilding my life again. Even though my phone had been turned off in Missouri, of course, it was the same company that serviced the area in Texas. This meant before I could move back out on my own, I needed to pay off that $600 phone bill. A few months later, I managed to do just that. I got a small apartment not that far from work but within walking distance from a mall. It was not in the best area of town, but not the worst either. The apartments between the mall and me were pretty sketchy, though. I just didn't know that when I rented it. Things always look nicer and safer in the daylight. By April, I had gotten the phone bill paid off and the phone service in the new apartment, but still had some credit card debt I had racked up in this process.

To solve this problem, I got a second job at a high-end toy store. I'd hint that it's the one that played the Clocktower Song over and over, but I'll just tell you that it was FAO Schwartz. I'm a big kid at heart so having a job where playing with toys is actually part of your job description is a dream. We even had the new Atari handheld video game system, the Atari Jaguar. Since I would never be able to afford to buy one, it was great walking around playing it and showing others how to play. My job was so much fun! Quite the contrast from my serious banking job by day. This also kept having a second job from being stressful or a chore. I actually loved it.

In my quest for self-discovery, I also took modeling classes and became a model. I mostly did bridal modeling. This meant getting to wear wedding gowns that I'd never be able to afford in real life. Honestly, with each designer trying to outdo the other, the gowns may have been expensive, but they weren't always the most beautiful. Even if I could have afforded some of them, I doubt I would have ever wanted to wear them. I have to admit it was a fun thing to do from time to time. I may not have made a lot of money doing it, but I can still say that I was once a model. Though it was a long time ago.

Life was going pretty well now. One day I was in the break room at work reading the local paper when I saw the volunteer section. I didn't know that newspapers even had this section. In it was the local rape crisis center looking for volunteers. I instantly knew what I needed to do. Since I believe that everything happens for a reason, I just knew I had gone through my attacks because I was strong enough to take it and survive and even thrive. Now I needed to help others to do the same.

I contacted the rape crisis center, and they gave me the training to become a rape crisis counselor. Once out of training, I would meet victims at the hospital and help them as they just survived the worst trauma of their lives. They didn't call us; the hospital did. We wore a pager, and when it went off, we had 30 minutes to get to the hospital. I don't think I ever had a call come in before 1:00 am, and most were between 2:00 am and 3:00 am. We would also be there if they wanted or needed us during their legal process, should they choose to pursue it. I still wonder, what are the odds that this was the only time I have ever seen this section in the paper, and the crisis center happened to be advertising for help that day? I can only hope and pray that I was helpful to the victims in their hour of need. I also hope they went on to get the full counseling they will have needed and then went on to have very successful lives. Sadly, I didn't get to stay in touch with them after the first few weeks or so, though.

Living in the Dallas area also gave me so many opportunities to experience new and interesting things. I went to places like Deep Ellum, car shows, the Texas State Fair, Six Flags Over Texas, the West End, plays, concerts, sporting events, etc. Living near a big city was awesome for someone in their early 20s. I went out on weekends with work friends but hadn't really developed any true friends outside of work yet. Sam came to visit me a couple of times, and Steve came to visit me a couple of times as well. I loved showing off all the things to do in Dallas to my friends. Secretly I was trying to get them to move down here. One place we used to go to a lot was a bar with a decent dance floor called Cadillac Jacks. I thought it was named for a guy named Jack who liked Cadillacs. I would learn many years later that it was named for a cowboy rodeo star from the 1960s who went by the name Cadillac Jack. How I learned that is a fun story for later.

All of this was not something I had not been able to do in the past. My past had forced me to grow up way too fast and kept me from being a normal young adult. For the first time, I was finally starting to enjoy this time in my life. I was still overly mature for my age, but then again, I was overly mature for my age when I was 10! At least I was now living my life from day to day instead of crisis to crisis.

One time when Sam came down for a visit, I took him to a Mannheim Steamroller concert. It was at an outdoor concert venue at Fair Park. We had so much fun! He had never heard them and loved them so much we went to the mall the next day and he bought 3-4 of their CDs. I was so excited that I got to add something new to his life that he loved. I thought his visits would have been more regular because he fell in love with Dallas and with Taco Bueno. (Taco Bueno is like Taco Bell, but better.) He never thought anything would be better than Taco Bell, but his mind was changed the first time I took him there. I really missed his laughter and smiles.

One problem was that I was still repressing my negative feelings. It had become the way I cope with any issue by this point. That came crashing down one day when I had to have my wisdom teeth taken out.

I was just barely 23, and I had never had surgery or any reason to be put under general anesthesia up till now. My wisdom teeth were impacted and they had to be cut out. This all started out fine. Mom drove me to the oral surgeon, I went back to the room, then they put the needle in my arm, and told me to count backward from 100. Not sure I even made it to 80!

The next thing I know, I'm waking up in such a disorienting haze. My mind was racing, and panic was setting in. I lost it! I don't mean I was a little upset. I mean full-on shaking, crying, and hyperventilating! They quickly unstrapped me from the chair and put me in a room to lie down. This didn't help. They even had to pull out the spacers they normally leave in because they thought I would aspirate them. The nurse came in with a paper back and told me to breathe into it. That still didn't work. Another nurse came in and asked why I was crying. I said between sobs, "I don't know!" Then she said I needed to calm down as I was starting to scare the other patients!

Mom was in the waiting room and could hear me. The surgeon came out to ask her if I have a repressive personality. Not sure how she responded, but he already knew the answer anyway. Yes, I did! He went on to explain to mom that the wall I had put up to hold in all those negative emotions came crashing down when they put me under. When I woke, I was hit with a lifetime of negative feelings all at once. He said I would calm down soon, and I did.

Anytime I realize that I'm repressing my emotions again, and I do still struggle with that, I just think back to that day. It's a reminder of the damage I'm doing to myself. It was just a small setback, or maybe it was a good thing, in my quest to get my life back on track.

The only thing missing at this point was college. I did look into Dallas County Community College once, but with working two jobs and modeling, when would I have had time? I just couldn't work it into my schedule. I was too busy working to pay off debts and be the adult I was supposed to be. I tried once with a single class, but it just didn't work out, and I dropped it. I figured there might be time next year once I had all my bills paid off. Once again, I was wrong.

Chapter 6

Getting Lost

I was now so far from college, and I had gotten lost. I was busy being a responsible adult now. I was working so much that I didn't have much time for anything else, but I was determined to get my life put back together.

Over the next year, I managed to get all my credit card debt paid off by putting all my store credit cards in a box. As I paid off a card, I cut it up. I was so proud when I cut up the last card. Looking back, I wish I had made some kind of art out of those cut-up cards. My career was also starting to take off. Instead of college, I began the climb up the corporate ladder. Now, that isn't always a bad thing. College isn't for everybody, and I just figured I was one of those people. By now, I had been away from college for four to five years and had had no choice but to fully embraced adulthood.

I had left my job at the bank and was now working at a mortgage company, just like my dad. I was starting at the bottom as a loan processor, but I was good at it. The only real drawback was that it was pretty far away, so my commute was almost an hour each way. Luckily, I had many doors open to me because of how well-respected my dad was, and I wasn't going to waste this opportunity. Since finance had been a part of my life since I was a child, it just seemed natural.

Growing up, I would go into the office with my dad on Saturdays, so he could call slows before we would go and do whatever we were going to do for father/daughter day. I would play with the forms and ask him what words were and what they meant. Picture a little girl sitting at a table in the back room, surrounded by Barbie dolls like they are clients. I would help them fill out a loan for their Barbie Dream House or maybe the new Barbie Corvette. When I would come across a word I didn't know, I would walk to the front of my dad's desk and sit patiently till he finished his call. Then I would point and ask what a word was and what it meant. He always explained it in a way I would be able to understand. Let's face it; I had to be one of the only 9-year-olds anywhere that knew what collateral was! Dad's work would also be typical dinner conversation as I was growing up, so I was very familiar with the business.

When I was a kid, dad had to do his own repossession. Sometimes it could be fun, like when he had to repossess a motorcycle (I'd get to ride, too). Sometimes it could be dangerous. It even put mom and I in danger at least once over the years. In fact, there was one time that dad even had a customer that got so mad that dad repossessed his truck, that he took his girlfriend's car and repeatedly rammed it into my dad's car in the parking lot of my dad's office. When dad called the police, and the police arrived, he was still at it. The customer then threaten me and my mom, even telling the police where we lived and what school I went to. I was only about 10 years old at the time. The Kettering Police

Department then called the Bellbrook Police Department to let them know about the threat.

In my small town, the police decided they would be extra cautious and follow my bus to school and back home, as well as keep an extra eye on our house. One night a week or two later, our miniature poodle, Cindy, woke us up in the middle of the night barking loudly. Her hackles were up and just could not be calmed down. This was something she had never done before or since. She was an extremely well-behaved dog, so this is extra unusual. We did call the police, who came over and checked around our house but found nothing. We have always wondered if that particular customer was outside our house and got scared away by Cindy's barking. Good dog!

Back to the present. I figured I could succeed in the mortgage business through my natural gift for math and being very detailed oriented, knowledge obtained growing up, and the doors opened for me by being Dick Barton's daughter. It's true that college would have greatly helped, but it was getting further and further away. In fact, I had almost completely given up on it. I was forging my way without it, at least for now.

During this time, I started back to church again. It was a small upstart church that met at a local YMCA. I loved the pastor, and everyone in the church welcomed me with open arms, even with my past. One Sunday, as I was leaving our sanctuary after church, my small group leader and my pastor each put their arms through mine as we walked. I knew something was up. They approached me about taking over our tape ministry. What is a tape ministry, you ask? Well, thank you for asking. In our case, since the Sunday School teachers could not attend services, the church would record the sermon and give the teachers a tape each week. The teachers would then return the tapes the next week, and the tapes would get erased and recorded again the next service.

When I was approached, I pointed out that I don't just do jobs. I do ministries. The way it was set up, it was a job. So, the pastor and I talked, and I presented my ideas for a proper tape ministry. One that could actually reach people and help them. My pastor listened to what I suggested, and he was excited. Then he wanted to know what I needed to implement my plan. I said to start with, I didn't want any tape handed back and erased. Surely each teacher knew someone who could benefit from that sermon.

Our sermons were practical and applied to everyday lives, so that shouldn't be hard. Second, since the sermons were taught in series, I wanted to package them at the end of each series, including the notes worksheets we gave out each week, and sell them. Similar to when you go to a seminar or workshop professionally, and the speaker sells tapes or books. The only difference was the price. Back then, a tape set from a business workshop would run around $199, and I sold mine for $20-$30, depending on how many tapes were in the series. My pastor thought all this was great and agreed to all of it.

I'm happy to say that the changes made to the tape ministry were a huge success! I was even making money for the church. When I asked for a 3-to-1 duplicator, because it was hard to keep up with the 1-to-1 duplicator, I had one a week later. People were even pre-ordering the complete series on the big series so that I would have time to make them all. Our two biggest series were "How to Keep Your Profession from Being an Obsession" and "Christianity 101". We had several businessmen and business owners that would keep these series on their desks, and when someone would ask about them, they would just give it to them, then buy a new one for their desk the next Sunday. They did this many many times over. Lee's sermons were able to reach so many more lives this way.

This made such an impact on the church that they even invented an award that I have to say I'm the first and only recipient of... the New Wineskin Award. For those that don't know what a wineskin is, in ancient times, the container used to hold wine was a pouch made of leathered animal skin. These would wear out and leak; therefore, you would need new wineskins. There is a parable in the bible that states that if you put new wine in an old wineskin, the seams would burst and would spill, so you should put new wine in a new wineskin. As my pastor put it, I had made a whole new wine out of old grapes and put it in a whole new wineskin. I was always very proud of this award.

At this church, I also met Richard. The first time I met him, he was just visiting from college at the University of Illinois Champlain-Urbana, where he was working on his Ph.D. A few months later, he was back home again, and we started hanging out. At first, just hung out as friends. The first time he thought of me as more than friends was when we had a sock hop at the church, and I ended up getting a migraine. My mom happened to be there because she had been a dance instructor for Author Murray back in the day, so she was teaching us dances. Once I got the migraine, Richard and my mom took me back home to take meds and rest. He claims this is the first time he saw me as more than a friend, but still just hung out as friends. I didn't notice much different between us at this point.

Things changed again when I had gone to his apartment for his HOME (Homes Open for Ministry and Encouragement) after a trip another friend and I took to San Antonio. I normally went to another HOME group, but we would occasionally go to each other's group. I started getting sick while I was there, so Richard and his roommate drove me home. They just dropped me off and made sure I had anything I needed for the night before they headed back home. The next day I was worse and had a fever of over 104 degrees. Richard took the day to drive me to the doctor. I was there for a long time as I had to have chest x-rays and have them read before I got the diagnosis. Well, I had walking pneumonia. He took me back home, and I crashed on the couch while he was still there. The next couple of days, he came by after work to check on me and help me out. Weirdly, this is when he claims fell in love with me. Go figure.

We were quite scandalous in our church since we were openly dating. Somewhere down the line, it had become a tradition in our church to date privately. Many times we didn't know people were dating until they showed up at church one Sunday, engaged. Not sure how that tradition got started, but neither of us thought it was of interest to us. Richard and I got along great, and after several months of dating, we got engaged.

Funny story of how we got engaged. We had been talking about it. Then he started looking at houses. He was nearing 30 and wanted to quit living in an apartment. We had been looking at used homes first, then realized it was actually cheaper at that time to build a new one. Now we were looking at new homes. During this time, my grandma in Missouri had a stroke, and mom and I had gone up there to see her. Richard asked mom and I to stop and see a model home that was on our way home. We did, and I loved the floor plan. They were giving a lot of upgrades for free as a bonus as well. A week or two later, we went up for Richard to put a contract in on the house and the lot we picked out. As we were driving back to Dallas and our apartments, he looked over at me and said, "Hmmmm. I just bought a house. Guess I need to decide if I'm going to marry you." Now doesn't that sound romantic? Well, he did take the next day off to pray and fast about it. Then we began to look at rings. The next weekend he proposed.

This being my second wedding, my parents weren't going to help pay this time. That was fine. To help pay for the wedding, I again took a second job. This time at The Disney Store. Anyone that knows me knows that I'm a HUGE Disney fan (though some would say fanatic). I had also recently changed jobs, and I was managing the office of a home improvement company. This meant that I was working about 50 hours a week at my career job and another 20 or so at my second job. Add to that, planning a wedding and honeymoon, plus I was still doing the tape ministry. We were also building a new house! I was just a little busy. My main job was so supportive of me during the crazy planning stage, though, and they treated me well.

Now, as much as I love Disney, I did leave my job there before the wedding. That might have been a mistake. My career job started treating me very differently once I got married. The majority owner, Gus, kept firing the people under me, so instead of a 3-person office with me as manager, I became the only one in the office. He found it easier to just keep increasing my salary than hire any help for me. I had to do everything. It took a minimum of 60 hours a week to handle all the accounts payable, accounts receivable, payroll, taxes, insurance claims, lead dissemination, and, of course, financing. Once I came back from my honeymoon, Sterling, the minority owner, was constantly telling me that "Now that I am married, I was taking away a job from a hardworking man, and I needed to be home raising babies". UGH! By the way, his daughter, that was just a week younger than me and got married the week before me, was a CPA. I guarantee you that he wasn't telling her that. I'm sure he was cautioning her to use her salary to save up for a house and a nest egg for when kids came along. But I digress.

The straw that broke the camel's back for me was when Gus decided to wait till I was sitting on the floor one day, surrounded by files, and started yelling at me for something that wasn't even my issue. I stood up to look him eye to eye (he was only 5'6 like me) and told him if he ever raised his voice to me again, I would walk out that door. Well, about 3-4 months later, he called one morning, mad about something else, and decided to take it out on me. Sterling, was already there, knew what Gus did, and told me to take a long lunch before I make any decisions.

I went shopping where I knew there was a pay phone and called Richard to ask how badly we needed my salary. He just said I needed to work, but I didn't have to work there. Then he asked if I wanted to tell him what was going on, and I said no. I was still beyond mad and really couldn't talk. When I went back to work, I sat down in front of Sterling's desk. Sterling said that he said that Gus had talked, and Gus wanted to make sure I knew he was sorry and was going to call me once I got back to apologize directly to me. This didn't matter to me anymore. I was done taking whatever shit people wanted to dump on me. I had done so much for this company. Besides doing the job of three people, I had computerized the office and had Richard write a custom computer program to organize the leads generated at the home improvement shows and record what salesman it was given to, and even kept track of what invoices were associated with that customer. Of course, that was done for free too! Now he wants to take his frustrations out on me!? No! I looked at the calendar and said 2 weeks from that Friday would be my last day. I never looked back. They did try and call me a couple of times over the years to ask questions on how to do something on the computer, and I was still polite and answered, but I refused to go in and help them.

I'd like to take a minute to say what a big deal this was. This was what my counselor in Missouri was trying to get me to do. I found my voice! I finally had built up my self-esteem enough to stop taking all the crap that I had been taking for as long as I could remember. I stood up for myself. I cannot stress how important this is. We all have times we need to find our voice and advocate for ourselves and protect ourselves, and that's ok. If anyone reading this is in a situation where they need to get out of a bad relationship, are getting passed over for raises or promotions, or just need to draw boundaries with toxic people, find your voice. Stand up for yourself! There is no one who knows your wants and needs better than you. You have a voice. You just need to use it.

During this time, I was again reminded of my lack of a college degree. In fact, it slapped me in the face. Three months after we got married, Richard defended his dissertation and got his Ph.D. in electrical engineering. While I am very smart, I'm not at Richard's level smart. He's MENSA-level smart. I say this as someone who has struggled with my self-esteem most of my life, being with someone who is way smarter than you and who has their Ph.D. when you have no degree at all, it will definitely strike a blow to your ego.

I've never admitted out loud how sad I actually felt as we were walking around the University of Illinois Champlain-Urbana as I was watching all these kids taking photos in their caps and gowns in front of signs, statues, and buildings while beaming with excitement and pride. I was fighting back tears. That was supposed to have been me. I felt I had been robbed of this experience. A combination of my low self-esteem on the issue and his way of constantly making me feel beneath him intellectually became a major issue in our marriage that lasted throughout the entire marriage.

I had tried one last time to go back to college and registered at Dallas County Community College again with one class, and yet I still couldn't manage the time and struggled with the math, so I withdrew. This was when Richard and I had just started dating. Life just kept getting in the way. I truly thought that I was at the end of any chance I had of college, forever. Honestly, it just wasn't as important anymore. I'd never get my college experience back, even if I went back to school now. The days of walking to classes or comparing notes with a classmate, or just hanging out on the quad, were already a distant memory. I was a grown-up now and had to put my college dreams away. A sad thought for someone only 24 years old.

Chapter 7

Sightseeing

Life keeps moving on and on and on. Always thinking back to my therapist's question, "Are you living from day to day or crisis to crisis?". I can finally say I was starting to live day to day. There was no life-changing crisis, and I was now living a good life. The problem was that I had all those adult responsibilities of work, family, and bills. School was still out of the question. In fact, it wasn't even a dream anymore. I had just given up any hope of going to college.

After our first two years of marriage, we decided to grow our family. On our first month of trying, I got pregnant. I had missed my period and took a home pregnancy test, and it came back negative. I told my boss, who had become a great friend, and she said that didn't mean I wasn't pregnant. She suggested I go to the doctor and have them do a test. I managed to make an appointment as the first appointment of the day the next day. Guess what... Valerie was right. I was pregnant! So, when I got to work, I told her, and we kinda planned how I would tell Richard that night.

I started to put my plan in motion. I went to a bookstore

during my lunch hour and got a funny book on being a father. I wrapped it in a bow and was going to give it to him at dinner. Once I got home, I told Richard I wasn't up to cooking dinner and said we should go out that night. He said he wasn't really up for going out, and how about we just go grab McDonald's? I protested and said it would be better to go out to a sit-down restaurant. He still said no, let's just go to McDonald's. I tried offering other suggestions, everything from Chinese to Pizza Hut to Denny's. He shot them all down, so we went to McDonald's. While Richard was getting our food, I went back to the car and got the book, and put it on the chair next to me so he couldn't see it. Once he came to the table, I gave him the book. He looked confused at first, then asked if I was pregnant. Of course, I said yes, and that is why I wanted to go to a real restaurant for dinner. He said if I had told him why I wanted to go out, then we would have. Ummmm, if I tell you, that spoils the surprise. There are times I just can't roll my eyes enough!

I had what most would call an easy pregnancy. Just a little morning sickness in the first trimester. Well, more motion sickness than morning sickness, which lasted the first couple of months, and bad heartburn at night throughout the pregnancy. My dog, Sable, was so funny. I would typically get sick in my car on my way to work or when I first got out of the car. Some days I could make it all the way to work but would end up throwing up in my trashcan as soon as I sat down at my desk. Other times it would be so bad that I'd have to pull over and throw up while driving. One day, I was driving to work and pulled over to eat some crackers to try and avoid throwing up. The crackers worked, and I was able to continue my drive. In the back seat in a pet carrier was Sable. I was going to drop her off at the groomer on the way to work. First, let me say she never got sick in the car. She had been riding with me since she was a little puppy. On this day, though, she got sick for me. I got to the groomer, and she had thrown up all over in her crate. I thank her for taking one for the team and supporting her mom. What a good dog.

I continued to work for the first couple of months. As I started my third month, I was laid off. In fact, it was the day I had gone to the doctor during lunch for my ultrasound. I brought back my pictures showing off the first pictures of my son. A couple of hours later, my immediate supervisor (not Valerie, they had sent her to Shreveport that day) comes to my desk, hanging his head as he has to let me and two others go. It really burst my excitement about the ultrasound pictures!

I still didn't have a new job yet. It's very hard to get a job when they know that you will be taking maternity leave soon. Two months later, Richard's friend from college, Pat, introduced us to a new type of game called a Collectable Card Game, or CCG. It was called Magic the Gathering. To play, you bought starter boxes and booster packs to collect cards. From those cards, you can buy or trade with others to build the most competitive deck possible.

It was very early in the game's life. I think it was only the second year it had been out and was building up a following fast. Most who played did so at a local comic or game stores and at local tournaments. From the original set, there were six cards that were the most sought-after as individual cards, and the first five would go for about $100 each, used. The cards were overpowered and had already been removed from the latest version of the game. These cards were called Mox's, and there was one for each of the five colors. The highest card, The

Black Lotus, could go for $150 and up. These cards were often used as prizes for tournaments at the local gaming stores.

While those cards were no longer printed and in the new booster packs, there were many other highly sought-after cards still out there. We took a chance and started a home-based business where we would buy a case of boxes of booster packs. We would open every pack, sort the cards, inventory them, and then sell them on the internet. This was the early days of the internet, so I didn't have a website or anything. I posted my list of cards on newsgroups with their prices. People would then email me with their orders. I ended up selling cards all over the world. This was so much fun!

My regular customers would email me, and we would develop a kind of friendship. I loved the ones from countries like Singapore, which had the government telling all kinds of lies about the United States. A lot of the emails were about me dispelling the myths or confirming them. Since I also played the game, I paid myself in cards instead of cash. This was something I could do while I was pregnant and after.

A couple of years later, though, the manufacturer, Wizards of the Coast, decided that they needed to bust the secondary market and therefore make it harder for people like us to make money. They flooded the market with the current high-dollar cards, except the Mox's and Black Lotus, of course, so they wouldn't be worth as much. Well, they succeeded, and I closed up shop, but it also came close to destroying the game. To be a "collectible" card game, they needed to have people wanting to collect cards and to get excited if they were able to trade for them or finally have the four of a particular card needed for their deck. They wanted to build their dream deck. It wasn't exciting when they were easy to get. They eventually put the collectible aspect of the CCG or Collectable Card Game back in the game, but the game never was as great as it was in the early days. I really miss those days.

But back to the pregnancy. Wouldn't you know, that was the year it got very hot very early. Having a due date in early July, I knew I would be hot and miserable towards the end of the pregnancy, but no one warned me it would get to the low 90s in March and April! I was really not liking being in Texas at that time. I was struggling every time I had to go outside. Between the pregnancy and having asthma, it was a struggle for me to do things during the last trimester of the pregnancy.

Now, in case you didn't know, pregnant women have lots and lots of hormones running amuck inside them while they are pregnant. For this reason, I'm going to give any men out there reading this a cautionary tale.

This story actually starts before I was pregnant. I had seen a diaper bag I really loved back when I was shopping for a baby shower gift for a friend of mine. Of course, since I wasn't pregnant, I didn't buy it. I spent my entire pregnancy looking for one I liked as much, but nothing was as good in my mind. One day, when I was almost 8 months pregnant, I went looking one more time. I had spent the entire day going to every store I could think of. Nothing.

I stopped by my husband's office, but I had to stay in the lobby and call him because part of the building was a clean room. I was upset and crying because I could not find a diaper bag I liked anywhere. Here is what you do NOT say to an upset pregnant woman... "Don't you think you are being a bit irrational? You need to get a bit of perspective." For any men reading this - DO NOT EVER say something like that to your pregnant wife or partner. No matter how true it may be, just do not say it. No - I was not being rational, but that's not the point. When he said this, I lost it. Complete meltdown. Luckily his boss's wife had just had a baby herself, so he fully understood and told Richard to go on home and let me calm down. Lesson learned. He did not make that mistake again.

The diaper bag wasn't the last issue, even though I only had one month to go. Let me explain to you about my luck. If there is even a 1% chance that something can go wrong - it will! When we took our birthing classes, we had a hospital tour. They showed us the 12 labor and delivery rooms and the 3 older overflow rooms that they typically only use when they know they will need the Operating Room for a C-Section.

Doing quick math in my head, I saw that 15 patients could be in at one time. I asked the nurse, "what do they do if they run out of rooms"? First, she asked me what did I mean. I asked again what they would do if there were more than 15 women in the hospital in labor at the same time. She said it never happens. But knowing my luck, I asked one more time what the plan was, just in case. She tried to reassure me that she had been there for five years, and it had never happened. I wasn't satisfied, but she changed the subject. This becomes important in a bit.

As my due date was approaching, I had an issue that was when I woke up one morning with blood in my discharge. My OB/GYN sent me to the hospital since it was two weeks before my due date. Due to the hospital not doing one simple check for amniotic fluid and telling me I had Braxton Hicks contractions, they advised me to go home and soak in a hot bath to relieve the pain. I wasn't due for two more weeks, and they insisted I wasn't actually in labor. Well, that simple check that they didn't do was a major miss. I was in a lot of pain and took three hot baths. What they didn't catch by not checking me was that I had a hole in my amniotic sack. To do that test would have taken about five seconds and a single strip of Ph paper like we all used in high school science class. They didn't check at all! The next morning I'm in full-blown contractions with an infection, throwing up, and a fever of 102 degrees!

My husband takes me to the hospital and drops me at the front door of the hospital, then goes to park the car. The front lobby is also where the administrative offices are. Luckily, one of the administrators saw me and grabbed a wheelchair, and headed for the elevator. In the elevator with me was another couple going to the labor and delivery floor. Since I'm obviously in distress and the fact that an administrator is pushing my wheelchair, I am taken to the desk first. I'm patient number 15, and the poor girl in the elevator is patient number 16. This is why I asked! In case you are curious, the answer is they put a hospital bed in the nurse's lounge so they could still hook her up to the monitors on this floor. That day they had a record number of babies born. 36, to be exact.

Because of my infection and the fact that I had been in labor for 21 1/2 hours without making any progress, I was taken to the OR the use the vacuum extractor. Neonatal is there to take my son right away as they were worried about him being born with the infection I had. The anesthesiologist was also in the room, ready to knock me out the second he was born since I hadn't slept in almost 2 days. Once they checked him, they gave my son to my husband to walk down to the nursery, almost forgetting about me. I hadn't even got to hold him yet, and thankfully Richard pointed this out, but I only got to hold him for only a manner of seconds before the meds kicked in, and I was out. It would be four more hours before I would get to hold him. Luckily, he was a healthy 9 lb 2 oz baby boy with no complications from my infection. I had to be put on IV antibiotics for the infection, though. All that could have been prevented if they had taken two seconds to use a simple piece of Ph paper. By not doing this and then giving me the advice to take hot baths, the results could have been catastrophic for my son or for me.

Chapter 8

New Roadblocks

The next two years were so much fun. A new baby with all the fun milestones to photograph... and boy, did I photograph! I bought film in 4 packs with 36 shots per roll. I would hate to add up how much I spent in film and processing back then. Whatever the amount, it was a lot! It was worth it, though.

As Ryan was nearing a year old, we thought something was so cute. As I would sit and read him his board books, he would occasionally put his hands down, holding down both sides of the book. I would have to re-read those pages to him, pointing to each word. I thought it was so cute because it looked like Ryan was learning to read. Guess what? He actually WAS learning to read! I even wanted to make him a onesie that said: "Needs Input". If I only knew then what I know now!

Now, let me get back to a story I alluded to a few chapters ago. One day in 1997, when Ryan was barely two, I was reading our local McKinney newspaper. In it, I saw an ad looking for people to be extras in a movie being filmed in our area. I only had about an hour before it started, and no way I could get a babysitter that fast, and that looked like an opportunity I didn't want to miss. So what did I do? I got ready myself, got Ryan ready, threw my umbrella stroller into my minivan, and headed to the audition. Yes, I was the only person there with a toddler or any child, in tow.

After I signed in, I found out it would be at least two hours before my audition would take place, so I walked across the parking lot to Braum's and got Ryan and I an early lunch and ice cream. Then we headed back to the audition.

Ryan was such a good boy. It was almost nap time, and he had a big lunch, so he was really sleepy, but he just sat in his stroller and played with his toys, not making much noise at all. When it came time for my audition, I brought him in with me. They did give me some odd looks, but I explained about just seeing the ad and not wanting to miss out, so I had no other option. Then I auditioned. When they asked about any acting experience, I told them about what I did at Rocky Horror. When it was over, Ryan and I headed home. I did stop and let him pick out a new toy, as we had been out for almost 5 hours, and he had been so good. He definitely needed a reward for being such a trooper. Plus, the umbrella stroller isn't as comfortable or roomy as a regular stroller, and he didn't complain once.

A couple of weeks later, I heard back from the casting company. I was in! The movie was to be a Hallmark Hall of Fame movie titled, *Still Holding On, the Legend of Cadillac Jack*. (Remember the bar I used to go to with my friends, it's that Cadillac Jack.) It was starring Clint Black and Lisa

Hartman Black. Filming was to start in two weeks at the old courthouse in downtown McKinney.

Now, this was before it was renovated and had the asbestos removed, and had working heat. It was an extremely cold and rainy October. We shot for two days... and then I was then sick for three more days. As it turns out, they were impressed with me and my determination because of bringing Ryan to the audition.

They gave me the part of the court reporter in the first trial. That meant I got to have extra fun and have my hair and makeup done in the makeup trailer by the professionals instead of being responsible for my own hair and makeup. Since the scene takes place over multiple days, but all shot in one day, I was constantly running up and down the steps to the basement where I could change. We first shot the first day's trial, then change outfits for the second day's trial. After the director looked at the footage, we went to reshoot the first day's trial. UGH! More running up and down the stairs.

The extra's room had a portable space heater in the room, so it wasn't as cold in there, though most kept their coats on anyway. As for us in the courtroom, we couldn't have any kind of heater, coats, or blankets because they would be seen by the cameras. I was so cold. Luckily, an older gentleman playing one of the guards had a coat with his uniform and wore it in the scenes, so between takes, he would come over and put it on me.

Between takes, I would also get to talk with the rest of the cast in that scene, including Clint Black. I also got to know the script supervisor pretty well and was asking her what exactly a script supervisor does. She said she watches each scene very carefully, taking very detailed notes. That way, if any reshoots have to be done, everything looks exactly the same. I laughed and said, "Oh, you are the one that I try to catch the mistakes from". She just laughed and said, "Okay, I'll go ahead and tell you now, then. On the rodeo scene, I forgot to have the wedding ring on Lisa's finger." Of all the things to miss, I thought this to be the most ironic since Clint and Lisa were married in real life.

I was also in a few more scenes just as an extra, several of which hit the cutting room floor, but overall, it was a fun and very unique experience. If you look it up online to watch, make sure you have your box of Kleenexes. I think that is required at every Hallmark Hall of Fame movie!

During this time, we also started going to a new church. At the time, it was a small church of about 200 people, but growing fast. Even though we had a young child, we still made time to lead a small group. It was great being active in a church again. The sermons, like at the last church, were designed to speak to everyday life. They dealt with how to be a Christian and walk in faith at home, work, and in the community.

As my son, Ryan was turning three, I approached the church about starting a puppet ministry. I had always wanted to be a part of a puppet ministry ever since I was a kid. The church I went to when I lived in Ohio had one, and sometimes the puppets got to visit our house so my mom could repair them. Mom never allowed me to play with them or even touch them, though. I hated that! My solution... grow up and create my own puppet ministry. Since the church was growing and the children's ministry was growing very fast, it was welcomed. I worked hard studying puppetry and finding the right scripts. I built my own stage out of backdrop stands and sewed my own stage curtains. The ministry started off small, but luckily one of my puppeteers had experience as she had done some puppetry in college. I found some really good scripts for smaller groups and even could ad-lib with me as the human and Holly as "Cool Carl". It was so much fun!

In the middle of summer, as we were building our skills and working on our very first show, I found out I was pregnant. I was thrilled, as was my team. A couple of months later, we went to perform our first show, and I was hoping everything would go perfectly. Here is one little-known fact about puppeteering, as you keep your arm raised above your head, your blood pressure drops. My blood pressure was low anyway, even being pregnant. I got dizzy and almost passed out during the performance. Holly quickly grabbed my puppet and finished the show with a puppet on each arm as I had to lay down behind the stage. Luckily, we were in the final scene anyway. During the show, no one knew what was happening. When the show was over, the children's minister and my team checked on me. I was fine after I sat for a bit but realized I wasn't going to be able to puppeteer while I was pregnant. I could still teach, choreograph and direct the puppet ministry, though. We were a small team, so I looked for two and three puppet scripts that they could still perform, and things went well.

A month later, my life had major roadblocks in store for me again. In fact, the roadblocks hit me almost all at once.

As I said, Ryan was turning three. I noticed that you couldn't ask him his name and have him answer "Ryan". You also could not ask him his age and have him hold up three fingers or just say he was three. While unusual, I didn't think too much about it yet. He was so smart and was even starting to read. We knew he could read and not just have them memorized as he could read a new book too, as well as read signs on the road or businesses.

When I took him to the doctor for his annual checkup, he had one meltdown after another. I would get him all calmed down, and when the doctor would come back in and he would have a new meltdown. The visit ended up taking 2 hours! I had never experienced something like this before with him. The closest was one time when he was still two, and he had a meltdown over something small. A meltdown like I had never seen before. I had even called my son's doctor about it. He said for me to just watch him and see if and when it happens again. At the end of his three-year-old checkup, the doctor suggested we take him to our local school to get tested. The school? I thought that was odd, but I trusted my doctor.

When school started, I contacted the school to see what we needed to do. Richard and I had a lot of debate about this as we remember the stigma of being labeled a special needs child from our childhoods. But as parents, we also had to do what was best for our child. Ryan was put in the PPCD or Preparatory Preschool for Children with Disabilities class, where he was observed and tested. After the first 30 days of class, we had a meeting where he was first diagnosed as Hyperlexic or advanced reading. It is on the autism spectrum, but after more observations and testing, we discovered it was actually Asperger's Syndrome. Luckily, as it was caught early, he could have two years of therapy and teaching with the possibility to enter mainstream Kindergarten. I got him a little backpack and lunch box and drove him to school each day, and picked him up after school. He loved going to school!

Within a month, though, just as my son was getting settled

into his new routine, I hit the next roadblock. I was only 12 weeks along in my pregnancy when I started bleeding one evening. My OB/GYN said to meet her at her office even though it was after hours. We were supposed to be hosting a get-to-know-you for the church at our house, and it was too late to change things. I also had no one home to watch my son. My OB/GYN said I needed to find someone and get down to her office. Immediately I called my friend Kelly, and she and her husband said they would come right over.

Before they got there, Richard had made it home. Richard kept our son and babysat the other kids that came over along with Kelly and her husband. Kelly was upset that Richard let me drive myself to the doctor's office. For those having any thoughts or judgments of me going to see the doctor by myself, don't. I handle crises better alone. When others are around, I focus on helping them and making them feel better, so I tend not to focus on myself and what I need. This was definitely one time I needed to focus exclusively on myself and my body's needs. It also gave me some alone time to talk to God. I needed calm and peace at that moment as my stress level was quickly climbing through the roof.

By the time I got to her office, the bleeding had stopped, but I was not out of the woods. She did an internal ultrasound, and the baby was doing ok, thankfully, but I was going to need to come back in a week for another ultrasound. Since I had stopped bleeding and she said everything looked ok, I wasn't too worried. Because of this, my husband went ahead and traveled to California for work the next week.

I went to my appointment, but my OB/GYN was in emergency surgery with another patient, so I went ahead and did the sonogram. They said the doctor would see me the next day and go over the results. The sonographer didn't say much at all, so I asked if everything was ok. All she would say is I have to talk to the doctor. Hmmmmm. Then when I get out to the window to make my appointment for the next day, they just kept asking what time worked for me, not what times they had open. Ok, now I am getting worried. What doctor, especially a busy OB/GYN, wants YOU to choose what time is best for YOU and not the doctor? Usually, in a case like this, they are doing their best to work you in somewhere. This time I was in control of the time? Needless to say, this was now making me even more nervous. Not good.

I called my husband in California on my way home and told him what was going on, or at least what little I knew. While he said it didn't sound great, he said he thought that if it was really bad, they wouldn't have just sent me home. Ok, good point. He said he would fly back home if I wanted, but I was still telling myself there wasn't much of an issue. I told him he could stay and finish up his work out there in the main office.

So, the next day I went back to my doctor's office. Again, my OB/GYN was at the hospital, so one of the other doctors in the office took my appointment. She pointed out I had a slightly detached placenta and bleeding between the gestational layers. What?! Needless to say, that really scared me.

First, they wanted to put me on bed rest. I said that was impossible as I needed to take my son to and from school each day. This was a very critical time in Ryan's development, and he needed to go to school each day. The doctor pointed out that this could cause me to lose the baby. So here is the huge decision my husband and I had to make... keep me in bed to protect the pregnancy, but if we did, we would have to get me some help as travel was a big part of his job, and maybe Ryan not make it to school each day. Or, I would still stay off my feet as much as possible but still take my son to school as this time in his development could potentially affect him for the rest of his life, but it would risk the pregnancy.

In case you think I'm being overly dramatic, for anyone on the autistic spectrum, the ability to get the communication, socialization, and physical help needed at the earliest possible age has lasting consequences. We made the decision that we had to do whatever was needed for our son that was already here first. This meant that I would take Ryan to and from school, make his meals with the help of others, and have my mom or friends help with the housework and things like bathing my son, as I could not lift him in or out of the tub. I would spend as much time as possible lying on the couch or in bed. My friends, family, and church all stepped up and helped me out. I could not have done it without them, and I am forever grateful for all of the support and help they provided.

This was early fall when I started having medical issues. I was pretty much stuck in bed or on the couch. Back then, we didn't really have laptops, and the internet was still dial-up. Besides, the internet was not as geared towards online shopping as it is today. Even if I could have sat at my desk at the computer, internet shopping wasn't really a big thing yet. As the months progressed and Christmas got closer, I was starting to panic. How was I going to be able to shop for gifts? This may seem trivial considering what I was going through, but I had always done all the Christmas shopping for our family. I was even one of those crazies out at 3:00 am for the best Black Friday sales. Sometime around late October or early November, the answer came in the mail. Catalogs!!! My husband then called or got online and subscribed to as many catalogs as he could that would help me shop for Christmas presents. He handed me the catalogs and our cordless phone when he would leave for work. Christmas was saved!

In the end, everything worked out as it should. Ryan got all the help he needed at the school, and my second son, Justin, came into the world three weeks early at 9 lb 5 oz! While it had been a tough decision to have to make, I'm glad we made it the way we did. Ryan was able to enter mainstream kindergarten two years later while still getting all the Physical Therapy (PT), Occupational Therapy (OT), and Speech services he needed. Justin was just fine with no other complications. In fact, he was a little kid genius. Both challenging to raise in their own ways, but I wouldn't change a thing. I love them both so much!

Chapter 9

Cruising

Life, now, was hyper-focused on being a mom. So many fun, funny, crazy, or frustrating stories could be shared - but that would need to be its own book someday. I won't say life was easy, because raising a special needs child has its own unique challenges. Add to that a second child who was way too smart for his own good, and well, life was definitely crazy, but it was a good kind of crazy.

My older son Ryan was doing good in school, with only a few issues here and there. Nothing we couldn't come up with a solution for. One example was the fact that he still had trouble parsing language, so explaining something to him verbally often just went over his head. This happened on the first day of gym class in kindergarten. The gym teachers tried to tell the kids to run in a certain way, and my son wasn't doing it. He was running in the center and in his own way. He simply didn't understand what they were wanting him to do. So, they yelled at him, which made him have a meltdown, and he ended up having to sit on the bench outside of the gym. He came home so sad and upset, not talking, and couldn't really explain why.

My heart was breaking, not knowing what happened and how to fix it. He had basically shut down. It took me most of the night to finally work out what happened.

The gym teachers obviously hadn't read his file about his particular special needs. The next day, after I dropped him off, I went to the gym to have a talk with the two teachers. They, in fact, had not had time to read all the files of the students and didn't know he had Asperger's, much less that he struggled with audio instruction and also did not know what his abilities or triggers were. They really did feel bad about what happened the day before. They apologized profusely. Of course, they had thought Ryan was just acting up on purpose, which is far from the truth. In fact, most children with Asperger's have an internal need for rules, and not following the rules is simply impossible for them.

Because he is a visual learner, we came up with a plan that we would have one other student in his class be his "gym buddy," and they would always be on the same team, follow each other in turns, or be side by side in a group activity. Every kid in his class volunteered to be Ryan's gym buddy, but we chose Michael because he had already started making friends with Ryan, and he seemed to understand Ryan a bit more than the others. This may be because his dad was a Care Flight EMT and very caring. The two of them became best friends that year. (Sadly, he moved away the next summer. Michael was such a great kid!)

Around this time, we are also realizing just how advanced my younger son, Justin, was. Kelly had a daughter that was two years older than Ryan. At this time, the Harry Potter books were just becoming a thing. Only the first three were out, and her daughter wanted to read them, so of course, Ryan wanted too also. Not knowing if these were appropriate for kids this young, I started listening to the audiobook while sitting in the carpool lane for about 30-45 minutes a day. Justin was only a year and a half old, so he sat in the backseat in his car seat, playing with toys. I LOVED the books! I listened to the first, then the second, then the third, then started over again. By the end of my second pass, the fourth book came out, and I added it to the rotation. This is also when the movie was coming out. The first time we passed a poster for the movie, Justin looked up and pointed and said "Haggid" at Hagrid. I was shocked. He had figured out who the character was by listening to the audiobooks! (Hagrid became Justin's favorite character. Later he would take a solid plastic Hagrid action figure to bed with him.)

Another thing that tipped us off to how smart Justin was came the next year we started doing flashcards with Ryan for math. Justin had not yet been to any kind of preschool or Mother's Day out program. That didn't matter, he was still answering the math problems faster than Ryan! Remember, they are only two months shy of being four years apart in age. This means Justin was answering math flashcards at 2 years old! While this sounds fun and like something to brag about and believe me, I did; little did I know what kinds of challenges a child that smart would be to raise. I do want to say here that this description is not to in any way compare the two or say that one child is any better than the other. Far from it. They are both amazing in their own ways. But raising each of them came with its own unique set of challenges, and I just want to let you all know what challenges we were facing at this point in life. Also, if anyone reading this has a child with either of these two issues, they may feel comforted that they are not alone. I'm not an expert on raising a special needs child. What I learned I learned by trial and error, and now 27 years of experience.

Because Ryan had social and communication issues, he struggled with making friends. This is why I made sure his parties were the best they could be. Some might even say epic. His birthday is in June, and Justin's in April, which means I started working on birthday parties in January! (Sometimes even earlier.) I wanted to make sure that kids wanted to come, even if their reason was the party and not necessarily to celebrate with my son. Take the wins you can get. I'll give two examples just for context.

When Ryan was in first grade, I threw him a Harry Potter party. This one I actually started working on the beginning of November! Since Harry Potter was such a popular costume that year, there were all kinds of Halloween trick-or-trick bags for it. After Halloween, I bought 25 of the bags at .12 each. In the spring, the Warner Brothers store was closing, and I was able to pick up all kinds of things at a super discount. I bought 20 sorting hat keychains, 20 little notebooks with the Hogwarts crest on them, stickers, etc. On eBay, I found a lot with 25 each of the *Quidditch Through the Ages* and *Care of Magical Creatures* books that were created for Comic Relief in the UK. I had individual boxes of Bertie Botts Every Flavor Beans as well. Next, I made wands out of the large pretzel sticks dipped in either white chocolate or milk chocolate and all kinds of sprinkles or colored sugars. No two looked alike. A glass jar filled with lemon drops (Dumbledore's favorite snack) was one of the things designed for the party. I found and ordered those little chenille worms that you can pull along your arm and around objects with fishing wire. For those who grew up in the 70s, they were the hot toy you could buy and find cheap smaller knock-off versions of in-quarter machines. These were like the quarter machine ones. The last thing was a magic trick to make a light bulb light up. Now I'm set. Let's get this party started!

On the day of the party, I dressed as Professor McGonagall and hung a Hogwarts crest on the front door. Each kid was given a name tag and a book bag (the Halloween bag), and they sat on the couch waiting for the other kids to arrive.

Once we had them all there, we had a wand-choosing ceremony where each kid would choose their wand - or the wand would choose them for those reading that knows the story. After that, each child would need to be sorted. One at a time, they pulled out their sorting hat keychain from their bag and flipped it over for me to see and read off what house they were sorted into. The keychains were sorting hats with a magic 8-ball like bottom. When flipped over, it gave the name of a house. Then I put a sticker on their name tag to indicate which house they were in.

Next up, charms class. They were given a couple of minutes to examine the lightbulb. Then one by one, they said "Lumos" and tapped the bulb with their wand. Points are given to those that figured out the trick (and about 5 of them did). Following that was the care of magical creatures' class. I had them pull out their *Care of Magical Creatures* textbooks from the bag and gave them their first creature to try and train and care for. That was those little chenille worms. They had fun learning how to make it move up and down their arms and through their fingers. The last class before moving to the Great Hall for the cake was transfiguration class. Here they transfigured the contents of a zip lock bag containing milk, cream, sugar, and in a separate bag inside that one, rock salt into ice cream.

Then in the Great Hall (dinette table), I had the Bertie Botts beans at each place while I served the cake, and they ate the ice cream they made. The kids found out that besides the regular flavors, there were flavors like grass and vomit in each box. They had so much fun challenging each other to try them. (Boys can be so gross!) Then I told them there was one final class, and that was divination. I put the jar of lemon drops in the center of the table, and they were to use their powers of divination to figure out how many lemon drops were in the jar. Prize to the one that got the closest. Ohhhh the logic some tried to use at such a young age! Then they all played with the rest of the stuff in their bags till the parents came to pick them up. Everyone had so much fun, and Ryan had gotten to dress up as Harry Potter for the party. Still one of the best parties I have ever thrown!

In second place for the most epic birthday party was the Teenage Mutant Ninja Turtle Party I threw one year. I'm not even exactly sure which child I did this one for, but pretty sure it was Ryan. It could have been Justin, though. I have a 50/50 shot at getting it right.

Since the show was just coming back on TV, there were no party supplies out yet. No problem. By now, the internet is where I can find just about anything I need. I made placemats by printing out one of the photos and laminating them. Found a Teenage Mutant Turtle cake pan from back in the 80s or early 90s on eBay. Kelly's husband had a second job at Pizza Hut, and he would bring me a few small pizza boxes each week. I basically lived on eBay, looking for cool stuff and finding activities to tie into the turtles. It worked! I found 50 book covers that had been promos for the latest tv show on FOX. My biggest score, though, was a set of 25 each of four graphic novels of the Teenage Mutant Ninja Turtles for a total of 100 books, and I paid like $30 with shipping! Found other little items from past party sets on eBay too. On the Nickelodeon website, I found the recipe for their trademark slime. Bonus! Once I had that recipe, I ordered several of the old action figures. We had a pizza party outside because, for those that don't know, pizza is the Teenage Mutant Ninja Turtle's favorite food. Then I filled a galvanized tub with the slime and action figures, and the kids had to go bobbing for turtles in the ooze (ooze is what made ordinary turtles into the Teenage Mutant Ninja Turtles).

When the party was over, instead of a loot bag, they each got a pizza box with one each of the books, a few of the book covers, and various other things. The boys were so happy! As one boy was walking out the door with his parent, he turned around and said to me, "Mrs. Burch, you throw the best parties", then flashed me a big smile. That is a compliment that I will forever remember and cherish.

Now, life wasn't all just parties and playtime. I was still directing the puppet ministry, and even took us to a competition where we won a silver medal. When our church was one of the first churches joining together to put on the first Clothe-A-Child in our area, I brought the puppets to put on shows and entertain the kids while their parents were waiting in line. Clothe-A-Child is a program where our church and a few other local churches made a deal with a local clothing retailer. They would sell us a $200 gift card to use for each family at a 20% discount. They would then open their store at 6 am on a Saturday, and we could take each of the families through and help them pick out clothes and shoes, and backpacks for the kids. therefore, we needed a lot of volunteers as we had to make sure they didn't even go one penny over the

$200 but helped them spend as much as possible. This meant long lines, though. That's where the puppets came in. These kids had to get up very early and be dressed and at the store before 6 am. They were tired, and waiting in line was boring. I put on a show every 30 minutes and also let the kids see the puppets and touch them between shows. This went on for a couple of years before I had to step down from the puppet ministry because I just didn't have the time to commit anymore.

Ryan was doing a lot better and was still getting PT, OT, and Speech through the school, but there were still so many things we had to learn while raising him. Even before his diagnosis, at age two, he had started to get very upset when we would take him to the movies, especially in loud scenes. This even included loud scenes in Disney and other animated movies. He freaked out at the final fight scene of Disney's Hercules on his 2nd birthday, which was something he had never done before. By 3 years old, Ryan stopped wanting to go to the movies. This was actually a clue to what was to come, but in isolation, we just thought it was his age.

After a couple of years, Justin was wanting to start going to the movies, but Ryan still was not having it. We felt bad only taking Justin, but we couldn't just tell him he can't see the latest animated movie just because his brother refused to go. It got to the point we would have mom or Kelly babysit Ryan so we could take Justin to the movies. One solution we found the summer before Ryan's third grade was noise-canceling headphones. It gave him a sense of empowerment as he could control when he would wear them, and it would cut down on the noise. This was a game-changer. It made it so he could finally start going to movies again since he hadn't been going since before he turned three, and it helped him at school where he could put them on when needed.

He had also become terrified of balloons. To him, it was because of the shock and surprise when they would pop along with the loud noise. This one wasn't as easy to control as so many places have balloons for kids. Think of how many restaurants have balloons for the kids that eat there or have party rooms that families can bring balloons into. Even when you go to Disney World, one of the first things you come across on Main Street is the cast members with dozens of balloons above their heads for sale. Balloons are everywhere.

The year Ryan entered third grade, in fact, there was almost a huge issue when it came to balloons. Luckily his teacher had already read his file and had called me to see how she could best interact with him. I warned her about his intense fear of balloons. On the morning of the first day of school, the parents had lined the ceiling of the school entry hall with balloons. Over a hundred of them! The teacher called to not only warn me but give me the option to meet us at a different door so Ryan would not have to be traumatized on day one of the school year. The principal was amazing and noted that it wasn't just Ryan, but lots of kids have a fear of balloons and had them all taken back down before any kids arrived. One or two of the balloons had escaped and were up in the rafters of the cafeteria, though. Even this was too much for Ryan, and he was too terrified to even walk into the cafeteria. Again, the amazing principal resolved this by her inviting Ryan to have lunch together in her office. I can't say enough good things about my son's school.

Volunteering at the school was something I did on a regular basis. First, I was a homeroom mom each year. Other times I was just reading a book to the class, or I was helping to plan and put on our big fundraiser for the school. When I say big fundraiser, I do mean BIG. We would have a dinner, a live auction, and a silent auction. Each class would (not grade level, each homeroom class) make a basket with a theme to put in the silent auction. There would be a live auction for the big items, and smaller items and experiences were in the silent auction. We raised a lot of money to help improve our school. Each year two of our two biggest items in the live auction were a puppy with all shots, crate, food, and toys, and the other was a prime parking place that only the winner could park in the next year to avoid the carpool line. They would bring in $1500-$2000 each, but even that got eclipsed one year.

One year, we had the fundraiser at the Bill Bates Ranch. For those that don't know who Bill Bates is, he was playing for the Dallas Cowboys when they were winning the Super Bowls and championships back in the 90s when Troy Aikman was the quarterback. When Bill Bates heard it was a school fundraiser, he surprised us by showing up at it! That wasn't even the best part, though. He asked if he could add something to the live auction. He added a chance to get your photo taken with him – and the winner got to wear one of his Super Bowl rings in the photo. The guys went crazy. The winning bid was $3800, passing the last bidder of $3500. So, Bill said that if the other guy would do the $3500 he bid, they could each win a photo. I don't remember the final total for that year, but that was over $7000 right there! Thank you, Bill Bates. You are the best!

I think I practically lived at the school sometimes. It was worth it, though. Your kids are only kids for a short time in life, and it goes by so fast.

There was one small but interesting thing I did on a whim one day. Ryan and I were at the mall, and they were doing an audition for a new reality show called Tontine. For those that watched Survivor, you probably remember Boston Rob. Well, he was staying in the reality show world by creating a new reality show. Ryan said he wanted me to audition, even though that meant a lot of waiting. It only took about an hour before it was my turn. This first round was mostly an on-camera intense interview. They were asking questions that would bring out my personality or questions about my home life and whether would I be able to actually participate in the show if selected. I thought I did ok but didn't have much in way of expectations. Over 100 people were auditioning at the mall here, and more auditions were being held all over the country.

So, I did the audition, and guess what? I actually made it to round two! Unfortunately, that was the end of my reality show journey, though. I didn't make it to round three, and the show died there. If nothing else, I can say I did better than most in my audition since I at least made it to the second round. Now back to my reality of being a mom.

Chapter 10

Breakdown

Sometimes we are just busy for limited periods of time. Sometimes we are busy because we have no choice due to work and family commitments. Sometimes we are busy simply because we use it to avoid things in our lives. That's where I was at this point. I had lost who I was and felt like I was breaking down. I masked this with shopping and volunteering.

My kids were getting older, and while both still needed me, the days of diapers and having to feed them were passed. Raising a special needs child and one that I needed to keep intellectually stimulated had me worn out both physically and emotionally. My husband was still traveling a lot, so I felt like I was a single parent most of the time. I didn't have the advantage of a work environment building my self-esteem by telling me that I was doing good and rewarding me with praise or raises, and didn't have anyone at home doing that either. I felt trapped in my house, and I felt so lost, tired, and so worn out. I needed a change somehow.

With some convincing, my husband finally agreed to let me

get a part-time job so I could still meet the family's needs while doing something for myself. This helped me tremendously. Here is one very important thing I learned during that time. Having a reason to get dressed up and do your hair and make-up helps your self-esteem. When you know you look good, you feel good. As your confidence builds, things happen, like your attitude improves, and you become happier. You also become more productive. As a stay-at-home mom, I rarely did my hair up nice or put on makeup. My clothes were boring but comfortable. There wasn't time or reason to do more, and as low as I felt, also just didn't feel like it. It's a horrible downward spiral. Now I was feeling more confident and felt like I was important to someone as my salesman relied on me heavily.

I had gotten a job with a new home builder as a sales assistant. I was very good at my job. My salesman would give me more and more responsibility and projects to work on. We were in one of the company's premier subdivisions. This is the kind of neighborhood with big homes on one-acre lots and tons of upgrades. I also worked in an amazing model home! We had 6,000 square feet of living space with Viking appliances, every room you can think of, including a huge theater room, an oversized game room with a separate card room, and a hidden reading nook. We even had a wine grotto in the model! Outdoors we had a pool, fireplace with a tv mounted above, a huge built-in grill, and six doors that opened up from the family room to this outdoor living area.

My salesman and I were selected to be the sales team for this community. This helped to boost my self-esteem. I felt valued and appreciated. I felt confident in my abilities again, and I was rewarded for my hard work. I had great customer service and sales skills; therefore, my salesman relied on me a lot. In fact, besides the $500 spiff the company paid me on each sale, my salesman gave me an additional $500 out of his commission because of all that I did. Things were going great until... the housing bubble burst in 2008. All sales assistants in my company, as well as most new home companies, were laid off. My salesman went to the number two person in the company to get me back, arguing that the high-end customers were used to dealing with me and I was an asset to the company and to him. To my surprise, it worked, and I was back on the job. Well, that only lasted a few weeks. Soon other salesmen realized that I was back, and they all wanted their assistants back too. The company decided it was disruptive for me to be the only assistant allowed to work, so once again, I was laid off.

I took this very hard, though I knew it was through no fault of my own. I wasn't sure what to do with myself. Should I look for another type of job since the housing industry was not the place to be at that time, or do I try and find a company still looking for sales assistants? I ended up doing neither.

Instead, I jumped headfirst into the virtual world. My friend, Nancy, now lived here in Texas, not very far from me. She introduced me to a game called Second Life. Well, not really so much a game, really, but a virtual world where you could do anything there that you could do in the real world and more. There are all kinds of clubs, live performers, amazing builds to explore, and so much more! In fact, some universities like Purdue were even offering classes for credit in Second Life! I was having fun making friends all over the world. I was also hosting events at clubs inside the game.

Now, here is also where things take another huge turn. As I said, everything you do in the real world, you can do in Second Life (and other games like it). I did things in the game and acted in the game in a way that I'd never do in real life. I really struggled with it and even wrote a poem about it, which I'll add at the end of this book. Feeling alone, frustrated, and unappreciated in my marriage, I got into online relationships inside the game. They treated me with respect and made me feel special. My self-esteem was craving this as it was back down near rock bottom. This is not what caused the eventual downfall of my marriage, but it was a symptom of just how much trouble it was in.

I had already tried to file for divorce once before this but was convinced to stay till the kids graduated. By now, I was in a major depression. I was easily set off and yelled a lot at everyone, including my kids. (I can never say I'm sorry enough or make amends for the damage I must have caused during this time.) The solution, even before I started working at the home builder, was meds. I was first put on the highest dose of Effexor, which is a powerful antidepressant, and now that it was no longer enough, they added Wellbutrin to the mix. I became barely functional both as a mom and as a person. I'm not proud of where I went at this time, but my escape into the virtual world was the only thing that I felt was keeping me sane. I was a mess. I knew it then, and I know it now. I just didn't know how to fix myself at that time. Could I have gone back into counseling? Yes. Should I have gone back into counseling? Yes. Did I go back into counseling? No. I can't tell you why, as I had so much success with it in the past, but I was just so deep into my depression that I just didn't see a way out of it.

One thing that didn't help my depression was my back pain. I had chronic back pain anyway, going all the way back to that accident after orientation at Wright State. Now, one day I was sitting on the floor, and when I went to stand up – I couldn't. I literally couldn't move without intense pain. That was in January. It took several different doctor visits, x-rays, CT scans, etc., before they came to the conclusion it was a herniated disc. During this time, I was in constant pain. At home, I'd just lay on the couch in the formal living room and sleep or be on my laptop. I didn't even get up to eat as walking was so painful. Every morning and afternoon, I had to take the kids to school and pick them up. Sitting in the car was painful enough, but when I would have to put on the brakes, it was excruciating. I would also have to take my younger son to boy scouts each week, only to sit there in pain while he was in his meeting. It was causing an even greater depression and a sense of despair.

Finally, in April, after they diagnosed me with a herniated disc, I had my surgery. When they got in there, they realized it wasn't herniated but ruptured. I spent an extra hour in surgery as they pulled large chunks of my disc out. When they tried to bring me out of the anesthesia, I started to shiver convulsively. Not knowing if it was the pain or cold causing it, they put me back under and brought me out slower. I woke up with 12 warm blankets piled on top of me. I was so weighted down I could barely move. From what I understand, the medical staff had all been really worried about me. Richard didn't go with me to the hospital. He said he hated hospitals, so he would stay home with the kids (something my parents could have easily done). My parents were the ones that ended up taking me to the hospital, staying with me during the surgery, worried when it was taking 2 hours longer, and picking me up the next day. This really bothered me and was probably the straw that broke the camel's back in my marriage.

One day I just kinda snapped and needed out. I decided the only way to save myself was divorce. I made an appointment with a friend of mine who was an attorney and set things in motion. A couple of months later, I was moving out and trying to figure out what I wanted and needed to fix the mess I was in. I was drowning and looking for a life raft but wasn't even sure what a life raft looked like, and therefore I couldn't see it.

The one thing I can say is that the kids remained the top priority for both of us. I may not have been the best mother during that period, but it wasn't because I didn't love my sons. I was just a mess. We split the time evenly and made sure each parent had time one on one with each son as well as time together. Eventually, as I got a new job and started to get my act together, we even set aside our differences so we could continue to take family vacations each summer. We also dedicated one night a week as a family night. We had a set of shows that we watched together each week as a family. We eventually added in Sunday nights as family movie nights because movies were and continue to be a big part of what we enjoy. There were also opening nights of the big movies we went to as a family. It may be a broken and weird family dynamic, but it worked for us. This all continues to this day, even though the boys are both in their 20s now.

Eventually, I started working again at a Texas-based jewelry company. Working did so much to help build my self-esteem back up. I was very good at what I did, and at first, I had a manager that recognized this and not only praised me but also praised me to others, even those higher up in the company. Eventually, I was promoted to the management team and worked full-time. This was the time I finally truly got my act together. I even went off all my meds and was just fine after that. I've never had to take them again.

The other thing I did was start my own website. My husband and I had traveled a lot during our marriage. I'm always a discount shopper, and it's the same thing with travel. I learned a ton of amazing tips and tricks to earn air miles; even without traveling and all kinds of free things you can get places. My friends and colleagues suggested I put it all on a website because they wanted to learn it all, too (and it's a lot). So, I did. In fact, I even started to create a YouTube channel. In case you are curious, you can visit the site at www.howtotravelfree.com.

Chapter 11

The Fork in the Road

Seven years pass, and with much hard work, I finally got my act together. As I said before, I got off both antidepressants and had I job I actually enjoyed. I liked it there, and I did well, eventually becoming a part of the management team. Even with all my experience in my professional life, though, I would never be able to be above the Sales Team Leader level. You had to have an Associate's Degree to be an Assistant Manager and must have a Bachelor's Degree in Business to be a Store Manager.

Now the time had come for my younger son to graduate from high school. He was all set to go to UTD, which is the University of Texas at Dallas. I was going to take his senior photos, and I wanted a shirt from UTD for him to wear in some of the photos. So, one Friday, which happened to be my day off, I headed to the University of Texas bookstore to pick him up a shirt.

I always describe this day as the perfect scene from a movie. It was a bright and sunny spring day with a slight breeze. You could see the kids lying on the grass studying and others walking to classes while chatting with friends. Kids were sitting in study groups in the student union, and others heading to the library to study for exams. As I got out of the car, I could hear the kids on the soccer field practicing and heard the sounds of music playing from one of the students sitting on the grass playing guitar. As I walked into the building where the bookstore was and looked around, I'm overwhelmed with a feeling of sadness and longing. I watched the kids shopping for their caps and gowns, trying on different sizes while their parents looked at the beautiful diploma frames. I bought the shirt and got back out of the bookstore as soon as I could before I started crying. This is what I had wanted. This is what I had missed out on. This is what I felt had been taken away from me.

By the time I got to my car, I was really crying. Not a single tear kind of cry or light weeping, but full-on crying. I called up my ex-husband, expecting to hear a little sympathy. Nope. That wasn't what he did. When I explained what I was seeing and why I was so sad, the only thing he said was, "So what are you going to do about it?". Hmmmmm, not the response I was expecting. It did make me stop and think, though. What was I going to do about it?

What WAS I going to do? Well, I had applied for and received a $5,000 scholarship from my company for my son to go to college, so maybe I could apply for one for myself too. Then, I applied to Collin College, my local community college, and was accepted. My company then awarded to me a $10,000 scholarship! That amount would pay for all my books, tuition, and all supplies and then some. I was blown away. I think I may actually be on the right path this time. Maybe. Of course, I have thought that before too.

Now for the scary part, actually going back to school. At this point, I'm 50 years old and haven't been in school in over 30 years. I wasn't that great of a student back then, either. Well, not because I'm not smart, but because I really didn't care about my grades back then. In high school, classes were just what you did while waiting for the after-school activities. Then in college, well, I just didn't have a great track record with my grades or staying in college. There was the fact that life had a way to keep detouring me from this path so many times in the past, so was that going to happen again? I felt as if I was almost tempting fate to try again. Also, would the students accept me at my age, or just ignore me or think I was a professor? Oh, and I didn't just sign up for one class, either. I jumped in with both feet and registered for four classes, all while working full-time and still making time for family nights and movies. Yikes!

As I said in my introduction to this book, this is also when I was having this weird dream. The same dream every night for five nights in a row of me giving the graduation speech. This happened the five nights before I started my first class. I had no clue why in the world I would be giving a graduation speech. I'm a nobody. I'm nothing special. Why in the world would I be giving a graduation speech? That speech stayed with me, though. I thought about it often. Parts of it would echo in my head all the time. The exact same speech every time. Very weird. For those that skipped the speech at the beginning, you will want to go back and read it now or after you finish the book.

So, I took my first four classes and was scared to death. My classes were all online, so I could continue to work while going to school. I studied at work during my lunch break and late at night, including after family time. If I had a spare minute, it was studying. I didn't even study that much when I was in school when I was younger, but I was determined not to fail this time. Lo and behold, I made the Dean's List my first semester! I have never ever made the Dean's List before! You could have knocked me over with a feather.

Second semester, four more classes. I didn't make Dean's List the second semester, I made the President's List! Honestly, I had never even heard of the President's List. Now I was on it! The second semester also added a new force in my life. Due to my grades, I qualified for and have been invited to join the Phi Theta Kappa International Honor Society. I was so excited, honored, and amazed to be getting to join an honor society for the first time in my life. Little did I know just how important this one decision of accepting my invitation would be to my life.

Chapter 12

Driving in Storms

I had my invitation for the Phi Theta Kappa induction ceremony and had RSVP'd for me and my family, including my parents. I have to say, I was so nervous. Since I was an online student, I didn't know if there would be any others there my age. I wanted to look nice, but not like I was trying to look too young, but I also didn't want to look my age either. I tried on dress after dress, and I didn't have anything I felt fit the bill. With my older son with me to give input, I went to the mall and tried on even more dresses. Luckily my son was very patient, knowing how important this was to me. Finally, after countless try-ons, I found one. This may sound silly, but I so wanted to make a good impression. This was one of the biggest honors of my life up till now, and I was so self-conscious about my age. I also had thoughts that, in some ways, it was a fluke I was even able to join. I was so afraid that I wouldn't be able to keep up my grades and that this would all come crashing to an end.

The night of induction had finally arrived. I had my whole family with me, my mom and dad, my kids, and my ex-husband. I tried to take in everything. There was a wonderful speaker that was a Phi Theta Kappa alumnus that spoke about how much being Phi Theta Kappa had helped him not only in his education but in his post-college career. There were also presentations on how to be involved in the chapter and so much more. Finally, the induction part of the ceremony itself. After explanations of what each of the letters and symbols represented, we were presented with a candle and white rose as we walked across the stage and then received our certificates. I'm sure there had to be at least a hundred of us being inducted! (Actually, I learned that it was well over 100!) Here I also saw that I wasn't the only "non-traditional" student being inducted, though I must admit not as many as I hoped to see. For those that don't know, a non-traditional student is a term used for us older students that have gone back to college. I was so happy and proud that I was smiling all night long. All in all, it was an amazing night. A night I will treasure forever.

At first, I struggled. One would probably say it was a bit of imposter syndrome. All these kids around me at the meetings were so smart and took such high-level classes. I had always been one of the smarter people around me, at least till I got married. My husband was a genius, and that made me feel very inferior. If I said something, it was challenged till I proved I was right, like I couldn't know something he didn't. Then I had a kid that is also a genius. While I am amazingly proud of him, I felt inferior to him at times as well. Now I had these amazing kids in Phi Theta Kappa that were so smart and taking much more difficult classes than me. I was just a business major. Don't get me wrong, there is nothing wrong with being a business major, but I couldn't take some of those high-level math and science classes, even if I tried.

Then I found my place. I began helping on the service committee by helping with the sponsorship and planning of CougarThon 2020. What is a CougarThon? Well, thank you for asking. CougarThon is a six-hour dance marathon raising funds for our local Children's Miracle Network hospitals. Having years of fundraising experience between church and the kid's schools as they were growing up, this was a natural fit for me. I also have a big heart for service. I have ever since I was a kid, and love being a part of something that could benefit children and their families so much. After raising a special needs child, I know how hard it can be on the kids and their families, and knew this is where I belonged. At the first CougarThon that I was involved with, we made over $6400, which was more than our college had ever raised before. On the night of CougarThon 2020 (luckily February 2020, before the pandemic hit), Dr. Hargis, primary advisor for our Phi Theta Kappa chapter, ask me to lead CougarThon 2021. Wow!

I was so excited. I started working on ideas that very weekend. New ways to generate funds, the next year's theme, and new places to get sponsorships from were all things I started working on. I got a notebook and started writing everything down and organizing it. I had a grand idea of making the theme Dancing through the Movies (working theme), and since we have Funimation, an anime dubbing and distribution company, right down the road, I thought of seeing if we could bring in some of the voice actors from big shows they dub, and since people usually pay for autographs, I would see if they would sign autographs and then would donate those funds, and then I could also advertise this in the local anime groups on Facebook and get even more people to our event. I also had the idea to see if we could get cameos from other stars and voice actors, many of whom I could meet and talk to about CougarThon at the San Diego Comic-Con that coming summer. It was going to be grand!

Then the world came to a screeching halt just one month later when Covid-19 hit. Nothing like a global pandemic to kill a perfectly good plan! At first, my advisors suggested I keep working on things as I had planned. At the beginning of Covid, they were thinking it would only last a few weeks to a month. When that passed, they then thought this would burn off like the flu does with the summer heat. It didn't. No one thought a year later we would still be dealing with it, though.

In time, we realized Covid wasn't going anywhere fast but still didn't think we would still be dealing with it by March, so my advisors and executive team suggest planning a hybrid event, so we could have fewer people gathered in one place, yet still have a large attendance including the online attendees. This wouldn't be as good, but would still be doable. Then by the end of 2020, we realized even hybrid still would not be possible. Our local Children's Miracle Network hospital insisted on it being fully virtual. Back to the drawing board once again to plan the event a third time, this time all virtual. Ok, now a big challenge, how do you make a *virtual* dance marathon? I'm not even sure the words virtual, dance, and marathon even belong in the same sentence!

This also killed off my autograph plans as well as a few dance activities, but it was still important to me to be successful and raise as much money as possible to help these kids and their families. Donations were down over 45% across the dance marathon network nationwide, and that personally put more pressure on me to make this as successful as possible. Time to get creative and think WAY outside the box.

You would think a global pandemic would be bad enough when planning something as large as this, but no. The universe wasn't done with me yet.

Starting on Christmas Day of 2019, my dad, who had been in and out of the hospital with a broken back and other health issues, was actually in the hospital when the first signs of the pandemic hit here in the United States. Things started off normal, and Mom and I would visit him every day.

There were starting to be stories of nursing homes and pockets out in California that had outbreaks of Covid-19, but just isolated cases here. Watching the news for daily updates was becoming the norm, and the talk of what was happing or possibly going to happen was a part of almost every conversation. Hearing the rumors of how bad it was in China had people nervous and/or scared. We thought we were pretty safe here in Texas, though.

One day, as things were starting to escalate, they stopped us at the door to take our temperatures before entering the hospital. We had been following the news and understood and appreciated that they were taking steps in keeping the patients and staff safe. Then the next day, they just didn't let us in at all. The hospital had been locked down. It's amazing how fast things progressed here. This was the same day my store had also chosen to close due to the pandemic. We all thought this would just be like a two-week closure, then things would go back to normal. Boy, were we wrong!

Dad really didn't understand what was going on. He had been in the hospital for the last couple of weeks and wasn't up on what was going on in the rest of the world. It didn't help that he wasn't watching any news while he was in the hospital. We didn't really talk about it with him before things locked down. We just didn't think it would be necessary. No one saw businesses and hospitals going on lockdown. Dad was upset as he didn't really understand why we weren't coming by to see him. This was really hard on my mom. Then he got transferred to a rehab facility for two weeks. We could take things to him and leave the items with security, then they would take them up to him. Again, he still didn't really understand, and I'm sure was upset with us for still not coming to see him. Once he finally came home, we tried to explain it, though I'm sure the rehab facility had tried to explain it to him too. He had to have noticed that no one had any visitors during this time, not just him. Once he got home, he didn't understand why mom couldn't just run out and pick up food or grab something at the store. The fact that everything was closed just didn't sink in with him.

Dad was now receiving physical, occupational, and speech therapy at home since he had been released from the rehab facility. He knew about Covid at this point, but I'm still not sure if he understood just how serious it was. A couple of weeks later, he got a really bad cough. By really bad, I mean very deep and constant. I told mom she needed to take him to the hospital. At first, she tried treating it at home. She didn't think it was Covid as dad hadn't left the house since he got home a couple of weeks before. It didn't get any better, so she agreed to take him to the hospital. Unfortunately, this would be the very last time she would get to see him alive.

They did not let her go in when she got to the emergency room. They met her outside of the doors with a wheelchair for dad and took him inside. At first, she waited in the parking lot for a few hours hoping they would give her an update. She had hoped they would possibly just be able to give him medications and send him home. That didn't happen. I finally convinced her to go home as dad was going to be staying in the hospital. Within 24 hours, he was on a ventilator and put into a medically induced coma. My family and I knew this was the beginning of the end, but mom just wasn't ready to believe that. Richard and I knew the odds of recovery at this point, and it wasn't good. We had discussed this with my boys as well. Later, they asked about doing temporary dialysis on him as his kidneys had completely shut down. I knew that this was the end and had already accepted it and, in fact, prepared for it, as I had heard the stories about those with covid this bad. Technically, he was not diagnosed with Covid, but that was due to early testing kits, but it was obvious that was what he had. They did diagnose him with pneumonia, but really this was just a secondary infection.

It was extremely hard, though. I have always been a daddy's girl. The evening mom had said they would do the dialysis on him, I went to go spend the night with her. I had only been there maybe 20-30 minutes when the hospital called that we needed to get there as soon as possible. Mom lived a good 30 minutes from the hospital. Once we got there, we had to first figure out how to get in as the front doors were locked, and the few people that could come in came in through a side door. Then we had to check in, have our temperature taken, fill out contact tracing forms, then be personally led up to the room. They said he passed away about 10 minutes before we got to his room. We had been at the hospital about that long before we were able to get to his room. Chances are that even without all those hoops to jump through to get in, we still would have missed getting to tell him goodbye, but we will never know. He never came out of the coma.

Due to Covid, we couldn't even have his funeral. It was April 2020 when he passed away, and everyone except essential personnel was kept at home. We finally put my dad to rest in late June up in Missouri, where my family's plots are. We had to keep it to a much smaller ceremony, though. At that time, Missouri had a lot fewer cases of Covid than Texas did, and figured this would probably be our only window to do this for a while. Not having the closure of a funeral for so long was very hard on mom. She was basically in a limbo of sorts. This was a lot to process during a lockdown, especially as she was alone so much of the time. I was back working with curbside pickup, but that did put me in contact with coworkers and customers. We didn't want to take the chance of mom catching Covid, so I talked to her on the phone, but limited my contact in person. Ryan and I would pick up groceries and Olive Garden for her but would drop them off in the kitchen while she stayed in the family room till after we left. We were doing all we could to keep her safe.

Phi Theta Kappa was what was keeping me sane during this time. Weekly zoom meetings and online fellowships kept my spirits up. We even had a version of Hollywood Game Night on zoom while I was in Missouri for the funeral. It made being there a little bit better as I had something to smile and laugh about, even if only for a couple of hours.

The universe wasn't done with me yet! In February 2021, about three to four weeks before CougarThon, a massive ice storm knocked out some of the power plants here in Texas. I personally had to go to a hotel as I had lost power at my house, which stayed out for a solid five days. The hotel also continued to have intermittent power outages, but it was decidedly better than my own house, which was freezing cold.

I went home a couple of times to check on my house. It was the weirdest feeling when I would get there. Starting as I got out of the car, it looked, sounded, and felt like a scene from a horror film. The air was so cold you could see your breath, and it was dead silent. Truly not a sound. You don't realize just how much white noise is around you till there is no electricity and almost no traffic outside. No kids playing, no hearing the sounds of the road off in the distance, not even the sounds of birds chirping or dogs barking. Nothing. The silence was deafening. Just the sounds of the wind and the tree limbs hitting each other with each breeze. I'll call it creepy quiet. If it was a horror movie, that's when the creepy music would start to play.

Inside my house was no better. It felt frozen (all puns intended) in time. Not a single sound except my alarm system beeping that I had a notification that my power was out and my battery was low. It was so cold inside you could see your breath in here as well. Nothing had moved, nothing made a sound, and no lights were on. Honestly, I was getting horror film vibes.

I was really concerned about pipes bursting. I had set all my faucets to dripping before I left, but they had frozen up anyway. Since I wasn't staying there, I went out and shut off the water to the house, just to play it safe. I had already seen several stories on the news of houses and apartments with burst pipes and didn't want to be one of those.

I was driving my dad's Jeep Grand Cherokee at this time. I had parked it in the driveway when I went to the house. There was some ice in the driveway, but I didn't think much of it. As I was walking out of the house on one of my later trips, I saw my Jeep starting to slide backwards down the driveway. Don't know why, but mostly because I was reacting instead of thinking, but I grabbed the grill of the Jeep to try and stop it. The guy across the street saw it and jumped in and tried to hit the brakes, but even the parking brake was already set. It was sliding, not rolling. He just put his foot down and held the door, trying to stop the slide with me. This worked. It had slid about halfway down the drive, but not into the street, and didn't hit the car parked across the street. Luckily everything turned out ok.

During this week, I did my best to keep having meetings on zoom as CougarThon was just a few weeks away, but my team's health and safety were much more important.

As you know, the show must go on. Luckily, we did get permission from the school for the day of the event that we could all be in one conference center room, where CougarThon was supposed to be held. We could be on our computers and stay well more than 6ft apart. This, at least, made it easier to communicate as we were putting on the event, so we weren't trying to text or private message during CougarThon. I had a lot of physical donations of goods, so I created an online auction. Using Zoom to make breakout rooms, I had a variety of games and Zumba classes, virtual karaoke, and Playlist Bingo, plus attendees could donate online to have one of the officers pied in the face!

All in all, it turned out great. We actually set a new record for donations from our school of over $7,051, all for The Children's Miracle Network! I had such an amazing team of officers, advisors, and members to pull all that off. I still can't thank everyone on my team enough for all that they did to make this happen.

I also learned one very important thing during all of my time in Phi Theta Kappa, and that was that my age didn't matter to anyone. No one treated me any differently due to my age. If anything, it was an asset as fundraising is something I had already done so much of in my life during my own primary schooling, in my church, and in my kid's schooling. I have to say that I also grew so much during this time, and it was all due to my Phi Theta Kappa family. Because of a shift in leadership about the time of CougarThon, I moved into the Treasurer position. Looking back on that year, the difference in myself between me at CougarThon 2020 and CougarThon 2021 is amazing. Even my family noticed the increase in my self-esteem and happiness. Luckily, my family is also very supportive of me and all the time I've needed to dedicate to school and to Phi Theta Kappa.

I can't say trying to juggle full-time school, full-time work, family, and Phi Theta Kappa was easy. In fact, quite the opposite. At one point, I thought I was going to crack. I remember curling up in the fetal position on the floor in my home office at 2 am, crying and trying to figure out how to get everything done. My solution, step down to a part-time job. It wasn't going to be forever, but this was such a unique and special time in my life. I wasn't going to let my college experience slip through my fingers again. I got a part-time job at the Disney Store. I had worked for them back before I got married and was excited to be working for them again. (As I said earlier in this book, I'm a total Disney nerd!) I started in August of 2020, just as things were opening back up, and we all thought life was getting back to normal. It was fun working there and putting smiles back on the kid's faces. Working part-time gave me time to dedicate to CougarThon, my classes, and other Phi Theta Kappa events. Plus, as a bonus, I was having fun. I call that a win in my book. Once the Disney World resorts opened back up, they gave all the castmembers huge discounts on rooms, and I was an annual passholder, so free to get in. Flights were super cheap to get people flying again. I took several mini-vacations during this time!

The pandemic had added a new stress to working, though. To open up, masks were required. The governor said everyone age 9 and up must wear a mask, but Disney's policy was age 2 and up. That wasn't just the stores. That was everywhere on any Disney property. One would think that after being cooped up at home and the holiday season upon us, that people would just be happy to be out, but no. Due to social distancing, we could only have 40 people, including cast members, in the store at a time. That meant we usually had a line, sometimes a very long line, to get in, especially on weekends. I would sometimes be the one controlling the line, making sure people stayed the required 6ft apart and breaking the line at crosswalks in the mall.

Besides chatting with the kids and parents, I was trying to let people know that a mask would be required in the store for everyone age 2 and up and that gators or vented masks were not allowed. I politely let them know we had masks they could use free of charge so that they could go in. Most people were fine with it, but there are always a few bad eggs in the world. I've been argued with, yelled at, cursed at, and some even took their kids away from someplace they really wanted to go, all because they didn't want to wear a mask for a few minutes in the store or have their young child wear one. This wasn't my policy, but they acted like it was. It doesn't matter what one's personal opinions are on a mask policy if those are the rules set by the company to enter. Either accept it for the few minutes of your life that you are in the store, or choose not to go to that store. We are just doing our jobs (and I'm referring to everyone working in retail or any similar environment). It is NEVER acceptable to abuse the workers for doing their job for which they have no choice but to enforce the company's policies, and that includes any policy, not just masks, unless they want to lose their jobs. I heard even worse stories from the cast members in the parks once they opened back up of being spit on or other abuses. I just don't get it. I will never understand why some people have to be like that. I didn't take it personally, though. It was just a small part of what otherwise was an awesome job.

Since it was just seasonal work, I was supposed to be done in January, and I had a part-time job lined up at the college in the office of Student Engagement to start in January. I thought it was a well-designed plan. Well, they kept me on at Disney till April, so now I was working two part-time jobs. Yes, I could have gone ahead and left Disney, but they were giving us such good deals at the parks that I couldn't leave. It allowed me to go a few times over this period. Even with both jobs, I still had more time for what I considered important. I had time for family, school, and Phi Theta Kappa, plus I loved what I did in both jobs. Still a win in my book. The mini-vacations to Disney World did a lot to relieve my stress and keep my mood upbeat. Okay, it was also so much fun Zooming in for a Phi Theta Kappa meeting from Galaxy's Edge (the Star Wars part of Disney's Hollywood Studios), usually in some form of Disneybounding, or with a parade going by. It was like taking my whole chapter to Disney with me! Disney World is definitely my happy place.

Chapter 13

You Have Arrived at Your Destination?

May 2021 arrives, and it's graduation time. At this point in the pandemic, some colleges were doing in-person graduations, while others were not. In my case, my college was not. I was so disappointed. I had waited so long for this. Now, I was not going to let some global pandemic keep me from walking across the stage at graduation - something I had been waiting 35 years to do. I had even dragged my classes out an extra semester, hoping that we could have an in-person graduation at the college. In fact, when I did my graduation photos at Disney World, I held a sign that read, "Even a Global Pandemic Couldn't Stop Me!", so this same pandemic wasn't going to stop me now. This was too big of a deal.

With the support of my family and my five fellow officers in Phi Theta Kappa, that were also graduating, we created our own, private mini-graduation. I rented a room in the historic courthouse in downtown McKinney and invited our families to the graduation. Friends and extended family were able to watch on Zoom. Earlier that day, all five of us got together and decorated the space. It was so much fun. We had a beautiful cake, and fun candy bowls with cute signs, like Smarties with the sign "Smarty Pants" and peppermints with the sign "CommenceMints", etc.

We also had lots of balloons everywhere. Even though it looked great, the limestone walls created one slight problem... the walls being stone kept popping the balloons. It was very loud! We invited immediate family to come to watch us graduate in person, and I set up a Zoom call for my speech by setting up a computer so other friends and family could watch. I also put a roadmap from AAA under each chair before the guests arrived, to be used during my speech. A graduation banner was hung behind our stage area. The room was so beautiful, and it was great fun doing it together.

The ceremony was just amazing. My ex-husband wore his Doctorate robes, and we rolled up certificate paper and tied them with blue bows for our diplomas. I started by giving the graduation speech, the very same speech you may have read during the introduction of this book. If you skipped to chapter 1 in the introduction, then take a minute and read it. (You can do that now or after you finish this chapter.) Unlike mass graduations where you are just one of the many graduating with just your name called as you cross the stage, ours got to be more personal. As Richard called each person's name, he told a bit about them, including their likes and dislikes as well as their accomplishments, and then where they wanted to go after graduation and go on to be after academia. It was so intimate and personal. It was also a unique experience that each of the five of us will remember for the rest of our lives. I will include a couple of pictures from the graduation in the photo album at the end of this book.

When I graduated, I had earned my Associate of Applied Science in Business Office Support Systems along with a certificate in Business Office Support Systems. After all, I had just gone back to school to do what I had been doing for most of my life. At one time, I had been running the entire office for a home improvement company or building forms and employee manuals in other jobs. Banking and finance were my specialties. Then after I took time off to raise my kids, I struggled to even get interviews for basic desk jobs, like receptionist positions. Even with all my experience, nothing. I knew I was meant for more, but for more, I needed a degree. So, I went back to school so I could do what I had always done. I was sure that once graduation was over, that was the end of my college career. In fact, when they filmed me at the end of CougarThon 2021, I was so happy over the amount donated and that we pulled it off after so many obstacles tried to derail our efforts that I was crying. I thanked everyone for helping and donating, then said what an amazing way to end my college career.

I didn't have any plans to go on to a four-year college to get my bachelor's degree, nor did I have the money to do that. Plus, with an applied sciences degree, I didn't take the necessary core classes to go on. That's what I thought my plan was, anyway.

After the graduation was over and the party was coming to an end, everyone was commenting on my speech. Many mentioned how moving or inspirational it was. To me, it was just my story, but I was glad to hear it meant something to them too. After we got things cleaned up and loaded in our cars, I told my family I wanted to go for a walk.

The historic courthouse is the center of the square, with a lot of businesses and restaurants surrounding it. It was a beautiful night, clear with a very slight breeze. You could hear all kinds of music and conversations coming from the bars and restaurants around the square, many with outdoor seating, plus a street performer playing on the corner. You could smell the wonderful food smells coming from area kitchens. On the square, you can find a steakhouse, an Irish bar and restaurant, a brick oven pizza place, and various other restaurants. I just walked, taking it all in. I had just graduated. But only to do what I had always done, which is never what I really wanted to do in the first place. I just kinda stumbled into this career. It paid the bills but didn't make me happy. Is that what I really wanted to do with my life now? Did I just go through all that just to go back to work in an office just to pay the bills? My life was so different from when I did that before, or even from when I started back to school, and now I wanted more.

I was now 53 years old and in a unique position in my life. For once, it was not about how much money I could make, but what did I want to do with my life. Would I like to do something such as work for a non-profit like The Children's Miracle Network? Did I want to go on to a four-year college like my classmates? Or, do I want to do something totally different? The world was now open to me to choose what I truly want to do with my life. To finally answer the eternal question, "What do you want to be when you grow up?". The answer was the third option, do something totally different. I realized that going all the way back to high school, I have always tried to encourage and protect my friends and later to protect and aid strangers. I have helped those that have needed me in their times of crisis and helped others find their voice so they could help themselves. So, what do I want to do with my life now that I have an open road ahead of me?

I want to continue to encourage, motivate, and empower others! It was then and there, an hour AFTER graduation, that I decided to become a writer and motivational speaker. I have been writing poetry and short stories for many years, now I want to write to help to inspire others. This book is just the start of my new journey to my new destination. A journey that I don't know what it will look like or where exactly it will take me, but I'm excited, and I look forward to it and can't wait to see what the road ahead has in store for me.

Chapter 14

Reflections

So, what have I learned on my journey so far? A lifetime of knowledge, for sure. But what are the most impactful things I have learned along the way?

If I'm being honest, there were times on this road when the answer would have been some very negative things. I spent a long time not trusting, not seeing the joy in life and in others, and not speaking up for myself. There were several years I spent with a chip on my shoulder and an attitude. In fact, Nancy once introduced me to her church friends by saying, "This is my best friend, Jayna. I'm so glad she's my friend because I'd hate to have her as an enemy".

I'm not proud of who I was back then. I was still helpful and caring to my friends and co-workers, but that's about it. It was hard for me to let you into my inner circle. If I did, though, I'd do everything in my power to protect you and boost you up. But even those dark times still helped shape me into the person I am today. With help from my counselor in Missouri and a lot of personal growth over the years, I am a much better person and have a very different attitude now. Thanks to my growth throughout my time with Phi Theta Kappa, I have set much higher goals for myself and believe in myself so much more than when I entered school. My answers to the question of what I have learned are now all positive ones.

Important things I've learned are that I trust that most people are good and do not say or do things deliberately to hurt or insult me. This allows me to give people the benefit of the doubt and not just fly off the handle anymore. Am I perfect at this? Of course not. I still get very hurt by people's words, but I do try and take a step back and look at the intent or motive before confronting them. This helps me not be as hurt or angry. The product of this is also better communication with people. Another benefit of this is that it also keeps my blood pressure and stress levels down. I don't look at the world as confrontational anymore. This helps keep me smiling most days, even on those bad days.

Speaking of smiling, I have learned to smile more. When talking to people, it's better to smile and be cheerful than have an attitude on my face. At work, I greet each student that comes into the office with a smile and a cheerful greeting. This often makes them smile. For those students that are nervous about starting college, it helps to put them at ease. I really like making people smile.

I have learned to be less hard on myself. I was always a perfectionist, but have learned that I don't have to be perfect all the time. Besides, some of the most successful inventions have come from someone NOT succeeding at doing something. Don't believe me, ask the guys that accidentally invented things like play-dough (supposed to be household cleaner to remove soot), the microwave (a radar experiment), or even penicillin (discovered when he accidentally contaminated his Petri dishes). Let's not forget the post-it that we can't live without. Did you know they were trying to invent the world's strongest adhesive? It's ok to fail. This is how we learn and grow, and I hope to never stop learning and growing.

Speaking of failures, when I do make a mistake or hurt someone, it's important to take ownership of that. I try to apologize and try and make it right. Whether at work, PTK, school, or family, it's important to own up to my mistakes. If I don't, I'm not respecting the others involved. Everyone will make mistakes and inadvertently hurt others. A sincere apology can go far to ease the pain. Then do whatever you can to make it right.

Fun is important! I try to add fun to whatever I do now. I learned that from my dad. If I find ways to have fun with my homework, it's more motivating to do it and not so much of a chore. Luckily, I have a job where creating fun is part of the job description. I've also embraced the fun person I can be and not being so serious all the time. I now have fun hobbies like going to comic cons and creating cosplay outfits. I love doing fun things like going to amusement parks and riding the big rides. Going to Disney World is something I try to do at least once, if not multiple times a year. I think, well actually, I know, I'm more fun now than I was in my 20s, 30s, or 40s!

I've learned perseverance. Things may not always work out the first time, or even the tenth time, but if it's worth having or doing, then keep at it. If you don't get the promotion you want right away, keep at it. If you don't understand a subject like math or science, keep at it and get help if you need it. If you want to take an amazing trip, keep saving so you can. If you can't go to college when you planned, keep the dream and keep at it. Never give up. Try and find different ways to make it happen. You may have to set something aside for a while, but that is not the same as giving up. I have a sign in my house that reads, "It's never too late for happily ever after". This is very true. If I had truly given up along the way, I wouldn't have graduated and wouldn't be writing this book right now. What's your dream? Always keep on dreaming. Keep going after your dreams and write your own story someday!

Looking back at where I was when I started back to school and where I am now, I'm not the same person. Not even close.

When I started at Collin College, I was unsure of myself and my abilities, insecure, scared, and suffered from a bit of imposter syndrome. I thought I'd just be a nameless, faceless student. Just one of the thousands of students at Collin College. Now I'm extremely confident, have a purpose in life, and have gained experiences I never thought possible. I'm no longer a nobody and even feel now like I am a person that could be asked to speak at a graduation.

I credit my experiences with Phi Theta Kappa for most of that! The friendships I built, the opportunity to do good for others, and the leadership opportunities it has provided me have shaped me into the person I am today. In fact, Phi Theta Kappa is still a driving force in my life as I have stayed in school to get "core complete" and go on for my bachelor's degree. Even my family notices the change in me since my involvement with Phi Theta Kappa and is happy with the changes it has made in me. Has it taken a lot of my time? Yes. Has every single minute been worth it? Yes. Would I be the person I am today without it? No. I'm so glad that not only did I accept my invitation and join, but I became an active member. It's true what my advisors say, the more active you become, the more you will get out of it. I have gotten so much out of it, more than even the advisors and my fellow members will ever know.

What is the most important thing I have learned? That everything does happen for a reason, even if we can't see what that reason is at the time. My assaults and how I've handled them have helped me to help others many times over. If I hadn't gone through the depression I did, I would not have gotten the help that ultimately made me a better person. It also made me understand what that level of depression does to someone, and hopefully can use that to help others. If I hadn't fought to protect others, even at a great personal cost, I would not have become the servant leader that I've grown to be. If I hadn't been forced to give up on college when younger, I would not appreciate the accomplishment that getting my degree is today. It means so much more to me now than it ever would have when I was younger.

If I had a time machine and could go back and change the past, would I? That is a question that I've been asked so many times. There was a time when I would have quickly said yes, but that would have been the wrong answer. The answer is no. I would not change a single thing in my past. This answer seems to surprise people. What sane person would want to go through all the trials and tribulations I've gone through if they didn't have to? Me, that's who. I am the person I am today due to my past and my perseverance through it, along with the lessons I've learned from all of it. Impossible to do without walking through that kind of fire. You can't make a diamond without a lot of pressure over a long period of time. Then you have to chisel it out, shape it, and polish it till it sparkles. I'm just beginning to sparkle, but I still, need a lot more polishing. So, the honest answer is that I would not change a thing.

If I could say one thing to anyone reading this, embrace

your past. Learn from it. Let it guide you to make better choices because of it. Become a better person because of it. Get professional help if you need to. Let your past be a guide to helping others. I truly hope you, too, can get to a point where you can say that you wouldn't change a thing.

Epilogue

The Journey Ahead

The nice thing about a journey is that it doesn't have to end. You just keep adding more and more destinations. I ended up staying at Collin College to get what is referred to as "core complete," as my associate is an AAS or Associate of Applied Science. This meant I was ready for the workforce but not to go on to a four-year college. This semester I am finishing my last two classes to have my AA or Associate's Degree in Liberal Arts as well as a certificate in Communications and will have the option to go on to the University of North Texas.

At the college, I have been given more opportunities for speaking and motivating, especially within our LEAD Program. LEAD stands for Leadership Empowerment And Development. We have a big one-day camp where we leave at 6:30 a.m. and get back to the campus around 10:00 p.m. It is filled with leadership-building activities and seminars. This year I was privileged to get to design and present one of these sessions. It was an amazing experience. Motivational speaking is definitely what I want to do with my life. Even more exciting was seeing people working on my handout after the session had ended during their free time. That made my heart happy to see that they got something out of it and wanted more. The presentation was on Self-Confidence for Leadership. I even suggested they get accountability partners and put the lessons in place for 30 days and see the result. A couple of the students were putting together accountability partnerships and groups. I could not have asked for a better outcome.

I have continued to have so many opportunities open up to me due to my involvement with Phi Theta Kappa. This has included having the privilege of running for International President of Phi Theta Kappa. I may not have won, but it was still an amazing experience. It has increased my friendships in Phi Theta Kappa beyond my own chapter. To this day, we still encourage each other on Facebook and I look forward to the day when I will get to see them again. I have also grown as a person due to the experience. Do I have regrets and things I'd do differently if I had it to do again? Absolutely! Am I happy with the campaign I ran? Definitely. Am I disappointed I lost? Of course. Would I do it again? Yes! It's an opportunity that came once and only once in my life. I've learned to make the most of such opportunities.

I have also had the opportunity to work with the president of the college and the web team in giving input on what would help the Collin College app be more useful and utilized by the students. First, let me say that when I started at the college, I would never have thought that I'd be sitting with the President giving my opinions on what would help the students of the college. Remember, I thought I was just going to be a nameless, faceless student among thousands of students. It was during one of these meetings that I expressed what I perceived to be a security risk on my campus (we have seven campuses in total).

The President agreed and made a call right after our meeting. Due to this, the college just spent close to $70,000 putting up new signage in our parking lots so that if you need to call the campus police, you can more accurately tell them where you are as we have several parking lots of all shapes and sizes. This will help the police find you faster, especially if it's a case where time is of the essence.

With both Phi Theta Kappa and with my job in Student Engagement, I'm getting more opportunities to present on topics such as professionalism and leadership. This will do more to prepare me for my career goals than any class I can take. I could never have imagined this is where my college career would take me. I'm still blown away by all of this.

Outside of college, I've picked up my camera again and started taking pictures. I will be entering some of them for publication in Forces, the college's arts magazine. Just before I published this book, I found out that one of my photographs was selected! I couldn't be prouder. The magazine will come out a week after the launch of this book. I'll post a link on social media and my linktree if you want to see it!

All in all, this has been the most amazing few years of my life. While I will be sad to leave Collin College as a student, it's soon time to set out on a new journey, see new sights, and have new adventures along the way.

Souvenirs of my Journey

As promised throughout the book, here are a few of my souvenirs from my journey to share with you.

As referenced in Chapter 4:

The Dance of Anger: A Woman's Guide to Changing the Patterns of Intimate Relationships

by Harriet Lerner Ph.D

Look for the Dance of Anger wherever you get your books from.

Poem (from Chapter 10)

Thru My Avatar's Eyes

What can we learn about ourselves
When we are not who we appear to be?
When the normal limitations in life
do not exist.

One would think that it's our personality that
survives...
but is it?
When we can be free of personal judgments
and society's norms.
Are we who we really think we are?

Who looks back at me
When standing face to face
looking into my avatar's eyes?
Is it the real me,
The me I want to be,
or the part of me I usually hide?
Is it possible to learn about me - thru her?

Sometimes I feel like Alice
thru the looking glass
living in a world that's upside down.
In some ways, she is the opposite of me...
in looks, this is most true,
But who she is, her personality and actions
should just be me as I am in control.
So, is she me upside down...

or a truer reflection of me?

Why do we all gather in a make-believe place?
So, the wallflower can be popular....
So, the shy can be outrageous....
So, the single can have a family....
So those confined can feel free in the dance...
or so the organized, scheduled, and most serious
of us
can find the fun in the last-minute spontaneous
activities?

Consequences - here there seem to be none,
So, we are free to do what we want to do.
But is this really true?
It's just a game I tell myself
and once really thought that true.
But behind every avatar is not a game engine...
but real people who play and laugh and hurt....
And I am one of them.

So, who looks back at me
When looking into my avatar's eyes?
A young girl who needs to grow up
and needs to realize that these are not her toys.
Someone with a lot to learn
and needs to play with care...
for the next toy that may get broken
is me...
or may be someone that I care for.

Photo Album

My school jacket. So many B's (you would think I'm good at sports, but I'm so not!)

Timmy's coloring book pages

My senior photo. It was taken the summer before my senior year started. The last real photograph before life turned upside down.

The Dayton Daily News March 28, 1989 and March 29, 1989

Mall-rapes suspect a sex offender

Loveland man served time

By Mary Sikora
Staff Writer

The 44-year-old man expected to be charged with raping three women after abducting them from the Dayton Mall was imprisoned for two years for kidnapping, robbery and rape in Hamilton and Butler counties.

Jerry Lee Bittner was convicted in 1975 of aggravated robbery and abduction in Hamilton County and of aggravated robbery, kidnapping and rape in Butler County.

According to Hamilton County court records, Bittner was sent to Lima State Hospital in May 1976 after being found to be a psychopathic offender. He was transferred to state prison in 1982.

Bittner, a short, balding man resembling the composites put out by Miami Twp. and Centerville police following the Dayton Mall rapes, stood passively before Judge John W. Wurts in Kettering Municipal Court Tuesday night as he was charged in connection with a February incident at Centerville Square Shopping Center.

Bittner was charged with attempted kidnapping, attempted rape, carrying a weapon under disability (because he is a convicted felon) and use of a weapon during commission of a felony. Wurts set bond at $500,000.

Bittner told Wurts he has lived in Loveland, near Cincinnati, for the past two years, is married and has three children, one of whom is still at home. He said he has worked the past four years at the Gesler Electric Co. in the Cincinnati area.

Centerville police Lt. Stephen Walker said the Montgomery County Sheriff's department has also charged Bittner with a weapons violation and traffic violations. These charges stem from his arrest on Monday.

Bittner is expected to be charged today in Miamisburg Municipal Court by the Miami Twp. Police Department on three charges of rape and three charges of kidnapping in connection with the mall rapes, township police said.

Walker said Bittner was captured Monday night when shoppers outside the Elder-Beerman store on Ohio 48 in Centerville flagged down a Montgomery County Sheriff's deputy after recognizing Bittner as fitting the general description of the rapist.

Both Walker and Miami Twp. police Sgt. Gary Williams say Bittner matches the description of the suspect in the

SEE MALL/5A

Jerry Lee Bittner

Wed., March 29, 1989 **Dayton Daily News** • 5-A

Mall

CONTINUED FROM/1A

Centerville and Miami Twp. incidents.

Deputy Michael Simms eventually stopped Bittner at Revere Village Drive and Ohio 48, saw he had a weapon and arrested him, Walker said.

Bittner is linked to rapes and abductions beginning in May 1987 when a woman reported being kidnapped at gunpoint from the Dayton Mall in her own car, driven around the area and forced to perform oral sex, police said. A similar case was reported to Miami Twp. police in June 1988.

The public search for a suspect resembling Bittner began Jan. 26, when a woman was once again abucted in the same manner as the other two.

According to the Ohio Department of Rehabilitation and Correction, Bittner went to the Chillicothe Correctional Institution in late 1982. He was paroled in October 1984.

According to an August 1975 *Cincinnati Post* article, Bittner was charged with kidnapping a 19-year-old woman from the parking lot of a Fotomat Store in Cincinnati where she was a clerk.

He forced her at gunpoint to move from the driver's seat of her car and drove off with her in the car. Stopped by the Glendale police for speeding, Bittner fled and led police on a high-speed chase that ended in Fairfield in Butler County.

He went through several road blocks and, at one point, tried to run over a police officer. Police shot Bittner in the thigh. He was later convicted of aggravated robbery and abduction in the case.

← Continued from previous page

March 29, 1989 ↘

Police may be holding suspect in mall rapes

Centerville police, responding to a suspicious-person complaint, stopped and detained a man Monday night matching the general description of the so-called Dayton Mall rapist.

An employee at the Centerville Union 76 service at Spring Valley Road and Ohio 48 said he saw a police cruiser stop the van in front of the station about 6:30 p.m. The employee assumed it was for a speeding violation.

"We didn't really think about it being him. We just thought it was another guy being pulled over," said John Wilhelm.

The van was described as a late-model maroon Chevrolet Astro van, which fits the description of the assailant's vehicle. The rapist's victims have described their assailant as a middle-age man with a stocky build and beer belly.

The search for the rapist began Jan. 26 when a woman was taken at gunpoint from the northeast parking lot of the Dayton Mall, driven through parts of Warren County and forced to perform oral sex before being released back at the mall.

At the time, Miami Twp. police said two other women, one in 1987 and another in 1988, had been abducted and raped by the same man under the same circumstances.

In mid-February, a man matching the same general description attempted to abduct a woman from the parking lot of the Centerville Square Shopping Center, near Ohio 48 and Spring Valley Road.

Graduation Photoshoot at Walt Disney World and Graduation Photos

In Memoriam

In Loving Memory

I've had so many wonderful people in my life who, unfortunately, have passed away. Each of them was loved by so many people, and I'm lucky enough to be counted among them. So many times, I've wished I could see them or talk to them again and often wondered what they would think of what I've made of my life. I would also wonder where they would be in their life right now if they were still here. I miss each and one of them very dearly.

I'm starting this list with my Uncle Jeff, who passed when I was just eight years old since he is the first death and funeral I remember. He was barely 28 years old and the best uncle I could have ever had! He also left the world too soon. As for the rest on this list, they are all ones you have met through this book. I wish I could say this is the whole list, but there are some not included on this list. These are just the ones who impacted my journey the most.

Jeffery Barton (Uncle Jeff)
Sept. 1948 - Nov. 1976

Timothy (Tim) Hicks
May 1967 - Nov. 1987

Kimberly (Kim) Williams
Dec. 1966 - March 1988

Samuel (Sam) McKendree
April 1966 - Feb. 1993

Willma Lee Hicks
January 1919 - July 2002

Shirley Hicks
November 1917 - March 2010

Stephen (Steve) Lilly
Feb. 1967 - June 2019

Gregory (Greg) Brock
March 1966 - Dec. 2019

Richard Barton (Dad)
May 1942 - April 2020

About the Author

Jayna Burch is a mom, writer, photographer, motivator, and now, college graduate. Immediately following her graduation, she took a long hard look at what she really wanted to do with her life and what she wanted her legacy to be. The answer was not to go back to pushing papers in an office but to do something to make a difference in people's lives.

Being very creative and enthusiastic, Jayna set out to become an author and motivational speaker. Having a very protective spirit, her goal in sharing her journey is to show that past trauma's do not have to define the rest of one's life. She wants to inspire others to overcome their struggles in life and persevere in following their dreams, and live their best life possible. Jayna does not consider herself a victim, just someone who had a lot of bad things happen to her that she had to overcome in order to better her life and achieve her dreams. She didn't just survive. She thrived!

Jayna is also service-oriented, innovative, and an avid community activist for children with special needs. She spent several years working with her area Clothe-A-Child and The Children's Miracle Network, as well as the kids in her son's special needs preschool classroom. Now she wants to focus her energy on helping other survivors live their best life ever.

For more information, visit JaynaBurch.com

Follow her link tree:

or click the links below:

facebook.com/JaynaBurchWriter
twitter.com/JaynaBWriter
instagram.com/burch.jayna
goodreads.com/jaynaburch

How Can You Help?

I hope you enjoyed following me on my journey. The road doesn't end here. I will publish more books and hope to build a community that can all support each other.

How can you help?

First, leave me a review! That helps me a lot and makes future books possible. The link for review sites will be on my link tree (see QR code above).

While you are on the link tree, jump to my website, jaynaburch.com, and join my mailing list. I'll update you from my mailing list on future projects, fun giveaways and let you know when the community function is active. I look forward to hearing about your journey!